Azure Cloud Security for Absolute Beginners

Enabling Cloud Infrastructure Security with Multi-Level Security Options

Pushpa Herath

Apress®

Azure Cloud Security for Absolute Beginners: Enabling Cloud Infrastructure Security with Multi-Level Security Options

Pushpa Herath
Hanguranketha, Sri Lanka

ISBN-13 (pbk): 978-1-4842-7859-8
https://doi.org/10.1007/978-1-4842-7860-4

ISBN-13 (electronic): 978-1-4842-7860-4

Managing Director, Apress Media LLC: Welmoed Spahr
Acquisitions Editor: Smriti Srivastava
Development Editor: Laura Berendson
Coordinating Editor: Shrikant Vishwakarma
Copyeditor: Anne Sanow

Cover designed by eStudioCalamar

Cover image designed by Freepik (www.freepik.com)

Distributed to the book trade worldwide by Springer Science+Business Media New York, 1 New York Plaza, Suite 4600, New York, NY 10004-1562, USA. Phone 1-800-SPRINGER, fax (201) 348-4505, e-mail orders-ny@springer-sbm.com, or visit www.springeronline.com. Apress Media, LLC is a California LLC and the sole member (owner) is Springer Science + Business Media Finance Inc (SSBM Finance Inc). SSBM Finance Inc is a **Delaware** corporation.

For information on translations, please e-mail booktranslations@springernature.com; for reprint, paperback, or audio rights, please e-mail bookpermissions@springernature.com.

Apress titles may be purchased in bulk for academic, corporate, or promotional use. eBook versions and licenses are also available for most titles. For more information, reference our Print and eBook Bulk Sales web page at http://www.apress.com/bulk-sales.

Any source code or other supplementary material referenced by the author in this book is available to readers on GitHub via the book's product page, located at www.apress.com/9781484278598. For more detailed information, please visit http://www.apress.com/source-code.

Printed on acid-free paper

Let this book be a daily reference guide
for all the teams who use Azure security.

Table of Contents

About the Author

 **Pushpa Herath** is a Microsoft Most Valuable Professional (MVP) in development technologies and an author, blogger, and speaker at technical community events. She is a Senior DevOps Engineer at 99x (Pvt) Ltd. She has many years of experience in DevOps with Azure DevOps, Octopus, JIRA, and many other DevOps tools. She currently leads the DevOps community in Sri Lanka, and she has demonstrated in-depth knowledge in Azure cloud platform tools in her community activities.

Pushpa blogs on technology, and has experience with Microsoft tools (C#, Azure DevOps, SQL Server, and Azure) and other tools (Octopus, Jira, BitBucket, MAQS, Sikuli). She has published five books with Apress and spoken at community events and published videos on the Sri Lanka DevOps community YouTube channel.

About the Technical Reviewer

Mittal Mehta has a total of 19 years of IT experience. Currently, he is working as a Devops Architect. He worked as a configuration manager and TFS administrator, and he is a Microsoft Certified Professional. He also has development experience in TFS, C#, SQL Server, Asp.net, Navision, and Azure Devops. He has been working in automation, software configuration, and E2E devops process implementation for the last 10 years in Microsoft Technologies.

Acknowledgments

I am thankful for all the mentors who have encouraged and helped me during my career and who have provided me with so many opportunities to gain the maturity and the courage I needed to write this book.

I would also like to thank my friends and colleagues who have helped and encouraged me in so many ways.

Last, but in no way least, I owe a huge debt to my family. Not only because they have put up with late-night typing, research, and my permanent air of distraction, but also because they have had the grace to read what I have written. My heartfelt gratitude is offered to them for helping me make this dream comes true.

Introduction

Azure cloud is a major cloud service provider embraced by many industries as the cloud platform of choice. Security of information, infrastructure, networks, and having compliance standards are of utmost important in cloud computing, and Microsoft Azure has a great set of security tools, configurations, and policies to comply with the required demands in the business world as well as governments.

The focus of this book is to help beginners who are moving to Azure cloud to understand the security concepts available in the platform, and to provide a hands-on guideline to set up security aspects effectively when deploying applications on top of Azure platform services as well as on top of Azure infrastructure. Fundamentals of Azure security are introduced, and discussion on management groups, subscriptions, management locks, and Azure policies further elaborate the concepts of Azure cloud security.

Azure Active Directory (AAD) and utilization of AAD in application security as well as infrastructure security is explained in detail in a full chapter. Essential aspects of keeping application keys, secrets, and certificates— which is really helpful for developers and Ops teams in configuring applications—is explained with regards to Azure Key Vault. The newest application security implementations such as utilizing Azure configurations, Azure defender, and Azure storage are discussed, and networking security aspects are described in detail for network security groups, gateways, load balancers, virtual networks, and firewall configurations. Creating more secure App Service Environments is further explained, and securing infrastructure is discussed in detail as well.

This book will be a useful reference guide for any beginner to get started implementing secure cloud solutions with Microsoft Azure.

CHAPTER 1

Understanding the Importance of Data/Application Security

Lesson 1.1: Introduction to Security

"Secure your data and applications," "identify security vulnerabilities," and "introduce security metrics" are few of the most common statements you will hear in any type of organization, and those statements always highlight the importance of security.

But what is security?

Security is a broader area that can be identified as the process of protecting data from unauthorized access and corruption.

Modern technological development has added more security vulnerabilities than ever before, due to the interconnected nature of the entire world. Stealing and selling personal data of social media users is a good example for understanding how security vulnerabilities have increased with modern technological developments. People are connected via the Internet and sharing data and information regularly, and without

© Pushpa Herath 2022
P. Herath, *Azure Cloud Security for Absolute Beginners*,
https://doi.org/10.1007/978-1-4842-7860-4_1

knowing they are doing so also sharing information about themselves, which may lead to security vulnerabilities. As an example, people share most of their personal details such as name, address, and workplace along with photos of themselves, and even share important life events to total strangers. The companies that own the social media platforms can sell such personal data of users to other companies and make money from it. A greater danger of sharing personal data publicly result in criminals using your identity for illegal purposes, which might lead to unnecessary troubles.

Considering the data utilized in modern applications to make intelligent decisions, there is a significant impact for tech innovations and the accuracy of decisions that can even cause huge damage to organizations due to corrupted or incorrect data. Artificial intelligence and machine learning are two trending modern technologies that train models using huge amounts of data to do specific activities or make predictions. Sometimes such predictions are used to make decisions upon medical conditions of human beings as well. However, if corrupted data is used for model training, the outcome will be a model that gives incorrect results. Companies invest large amounts of money to do machine learning projects, and therefore the accuracy and protection of data is essential to ensure that the successful machine learning model serves the intended purpose without causing negative impacts.

Phishing attacks are another type of security threat. In a phishing attack a human may be tricked into opening a backdoor to a secure network, or to deploy ransomware in a network, so that the attacker can use sensitive information to exploit the network and corrupt the connected machines, applications, and data. Figure 1-1 illustrates the range of cloud security challenges faced by developers and companies.

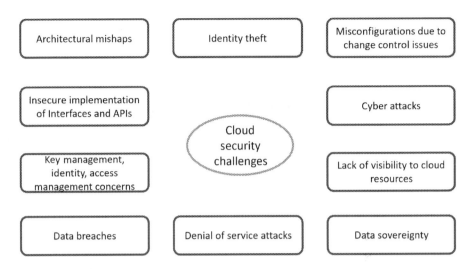

Figure 1-1. *Cloud security challenges*

Cloud computing is another well-known tech trend that allows customers to connect with servers established in a data centre by means of a public cloud hosting company. Such use of public cloud allows more shared infrastructure and interconnectivity. This is truly beneficial to increase the usage of technology with ease; however, such close connectivity and shared resources make the security risks higher as well. The public cloud providers take the strongest possible measures to avoid such vulnerabilities, but as a user of a cloud platform there is some level of security configuration responsibility assigned to the application deploying and developing companies, as well on top of public clouds. This responsibility matrix is further discussed in the next lesson in this chapter, with the example of Microsoft public cloud Azure.

The security process consists of multiple layers of security, including both physical and virtual security mechanisms. Installing security systems at the entrance of the organization, password-protected computers, or other devices, and even ensuring that individuals do not share personal and corporate details when having conversations with others, are important security components in the process of implementing security.

Most of the organizations have identified the risk of not having a properly implemented security process and are trying to add at least a few security gates to the organizations. However, with the fast-developing nature of the IT industry and technology, there are new security vulnerabilities daily that question and stress the existing security mechanisms. Therefore, it is mandatory to identify and introduce the security measures to the organization as well as to the individuals.

Did you know that data is commonly known as the most valuable assets of the organization? This is why organizations invest a decent amount of money for security.

You might be interested to learn more about how crucial data and application security is for an organization and what type of damage it can do to an organization when security vulnerabilities are exploited.

Failure to protect data and application add the following risks to an organization:

1. The organization could lose your money and cause other damage.

    With the fast-growing technology, hackers are also getting smarter every day. Therefore, it is mandatory to have proper protected systems. Imagine a situation where someone hacked into your bank account; you would lose all your savings within a few seconds. If the hackers were terrorists compromising an automated traffic control system of trains, it could lead to a disaster resulting in the loss of thousands of human lives. Therefore, security vulnerabilities are a huge threat to countries, organizations, and individuals.

2. The organization could lose the trust of its clients.

    As an IT industry employee, you are aware that you get access to a lot of client's data and applications. These data can be very personal details of employees, details of customers, or even highly classified data belonging to departments such as research and development or defence forces. Your clients provide access to such information by trusting your security measures. However, if you fail to keep the data secured, the trust toward the organization can be lost and may even result in lawsuits against your company.

3. The organization's brand name could be damaged.

    Organizations have built up their own brands and recognition due to the high-quality work, cutting-edge technologies, and challenging implementations. However, if your organization failed to embrace the security measures, you might lose the good name earned.

4. The organization's agreements with clients could be breached, resulting in legal troubles.

    If an organization fails to secure a client's data, this could result in legal battles with clients that might well end up with bankruptcy or even imprisonment of owners and shareholders. Recently, Facebook has gotten attention due to fraud on selling users data, which did a lot of harm to the brand name.

Now you know security is not something you can take lightly. You must take all the possible actions to ensure the security of data and applications.

You might wonder what can be done to increase security. Let's look at the options available. For the system development process, we can follow best practices to develop secured systems.

Introduce security components throughout the entire software development life cycle, from requirement gathering to monitoring and maintenance.

Identify mechanisms to follow in each step of the software development life cycle to make sure the security is enforced. Who has access to the systems, how is infrastructure to be secured, how will secure development code be written, and how will vulnerability testing be conducted? All of these questions need to be identified at the beginning of a software project development.

Introduce secure architecture to consider the tools and platforms that will be used for development. Where are the passwords and other secrets going to be stored, what database system will be used, what type of security is included in the database management system, and how will networks properly secure data and applications? All these questions need to be answered when the architecture is articulated (see Figure 1-2).

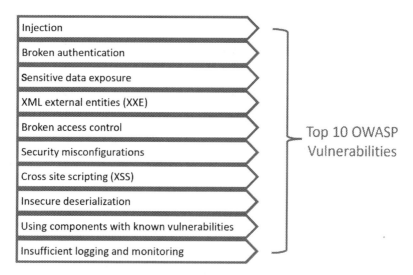

Figure 1-2. *OWASP top 10*

Proper coding practices, error handling, and session management also need to be considered while introducing the security measures. Introducing Continuous Integration and continuous delivery (CI/CD), scanning tools, vulnerability testing tools, and monitoring tools to maintain the security are important aspects as well. Identify the Open Web Application Security Project (OWASP) top-ten security threats and introduce security components should be practiced.

In this lesson we have discussed the importance of security to an organization. Now you have an understanding of why security is crucial, and a basic idea of possible mechanisms that can be taken to improve the security of the data and applications.

Lesson 1.2: Introduction to Azure Security Fundamentals

"Cloud computing" and "cloud platforms" are famous words among not only IT employees, but with the general public as well. It is clear that cloud technologies are emerging technologies that solve many infrastructure maintenance problems faced by organizations.

Cloud computing is the delivery of computer services over the Internet, which helps users to reduce operating costs, maintain and run infrastructure more efficiently, and pay only for the usage of service.

Azure is such a cloud service from Microsoft that has various services for clients such as software as service (SAAS), platform as service (PAAS), and infrastructure as service (IAAS). Most importantly in this lesson, you are going to have a quick overview of security components Azure provides with their wide range of cloud services. Security is considered a shared responsibility, and both service provider and client need to be committed to data and application security. Figure 1-3 depicts the shared responsibility model of Azure.

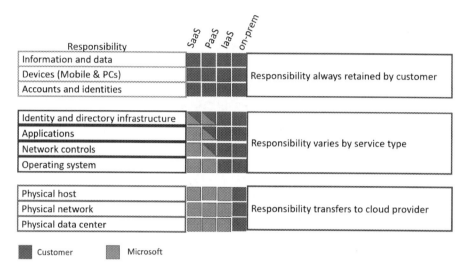

Figure 1-3. *Shared responsibility model Azure*

The cloud provider takes full responsibility for security of the following:

- Physical host of SAAS, PAAS, and IAAS

- Physical network of SAAS, PAAS, and IAAS

- Physical data center of SAAS, PAAS, and IAAS

- Operating system of SAAS and PAAS

- Network control of SAAS

- Applications of SAAS

Responsibilities shared between customer and cloud provider based on the service type are the following:

- Identity and directory infrastructure of SAAS and PAAS

- Applications of PAAS

- Network control of PAAS

Customers have to be responsible for securing the following:

- Information and data of SAAS, PAAS, and IAAS

- Devices of SAAS, PAAS, and IAAS

- Accounts and identities of SAAS, PAAS, and IAAS

- Identity and directory infrastructure of IAAS

- Applications of IAAS

- Network control of IAAS

- Operating system of IAAS

Now you know that security is a shared responsibility of both client and cloud provider. Therefore, it is mandatory to identify the security threat of each cloud service and apply the correct security mechanism to minimize the risk. Azure provides several security features to users to minimize the security vulnerabilities related to data and applications.

Azure security center, Azure monitor logs, and Azure key vaults are general security components available in Azure. Azure also provides security features such as storage security and database security. Access management is one of the main security concerns that can be addressed with Azure identity and access management features. Networking also plays a major role in considering the security of data and applications, and Azure provides several options such as application gateway, virtual networks, traffic managers, and firewalls. These are the few of the security features available in Azure that you will be able to learn more about in the following chapters.

We have come to the end of Chapter 1. In this chapter you were introduced to the idea of why security is important and how security can affect an organization, and to how it can affect society and business on a global scale. You have also been provided with a basic understanding of shared responsibilities of cloud security and security features available with Azure.

Summary

In this chapter we have discussed the importance of security in the modern cloud-based nature of application solutions. We have also briefly explored the considerations in Azure cloud regarding security.

In the next chapter, we will discuss basic Azure security components.

CHAPTER 2

Overview of Basic Azure Security Components

Azure is a leading cloud service platform that provides many services to implement modern cloud solutions. With the identification of growth of security vulnerabilities due to the development of technology and the wide adoption of cloud services, introduction of several security mechanisms in Azure is essential. You will be able to explore a few of the security components available with Azure in this chapter.

Lesson 2.1: Introduction to Azure Management Groups and Subscriptions

Generally, a tidy and well-organized room or work table is calming for users, and it helps them to focus on their work without having unnecessary disturbances or time-wasting due to unclean surroundings. The same concept is applied to the resources you use in your project development. If you keep your resources clean and organized, you can see the security threats of the resources and take necessary actions before your resources get attacked.

© Pushpa Herath 2022
P. Herath, *Azure Cloud Security for Absolute Beginners*,
https://doi.org/10.1007/978-1-4842-7860-4_2

Azure has several resource organizing mechanisms that can be used to group resources according to several facts. For example, resources that have the same lifetime are added into one resource group. This means that if you want to drop resources in this specific resource group, you will be able to delete the entire resource group without deleting them one by one.

In terms of the security aspect of Azure resources, Azure management groups play an important role. You will be able to learn about Azure management groups and how to use it in this lesson.

Before digging deep into the management groups, let's discuss how to get an initial Azure subscription.

Azure subscription is a logical unit of services that is attached to the Azure account. While you are creating your Azure account, you can select the subscription type you need. Azure provides several subscriptions that allow users to access several resources and manage the cost of resources according to the resource usage.

Azure subscription is not only a logical unit for billing purposes. It can also be used as a unit for securing and isolating the Azure resources.

You can maintain one Azure subscription for production environments and one for nonproduction environments. By having two separate subscriptions, you can ensure security of the production environment by limiting the production access for developers. Moreover, if you are using Azure DevOps to deploy resources via pipelines, you can create service connection scoping to a given subscription level and control the production and nonproduction resource deployment access separately.

Now you know what an Azure subscription is and how to use it to secure the resources. In the real world, most the companies use multiple subscriptions to manage Azure resources for different purposes. Managing such subscriptions correctly is mandatory in order to maintain the security of the organization. Therefore, companies use management groups to organize and control multiple Azure subscriptions.

Management groups can be used to manage access, policies, and compliance of Azure subscriptions. If policies are added to the management group, subscriptions under the management group inherit the policies.

Let's create a management group.

Go to `https://portal.azure.com/` and log in as an administrator.

Search Management group and click on the value in the search result (see Figure 2-1).

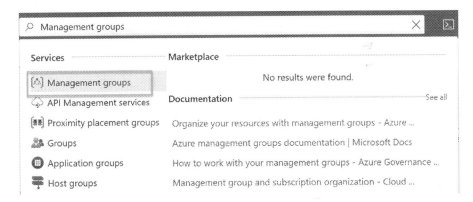

Figure 2-1. *Management groups*

You will be able to see the overview page of the Management group (see Figure 2-2).

1. Create new management group

2. Add new subscription to management group

3. Management group settings

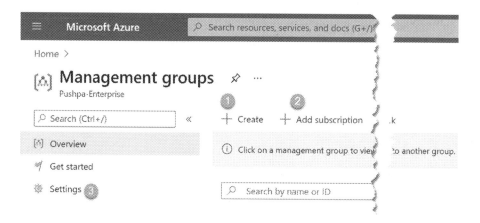

Figure 2-2. *Management group overview*

Click on Create, the first step in Figure 2-2. It will open a pane where you can enter details to create a new management group (see Figure 2-3).

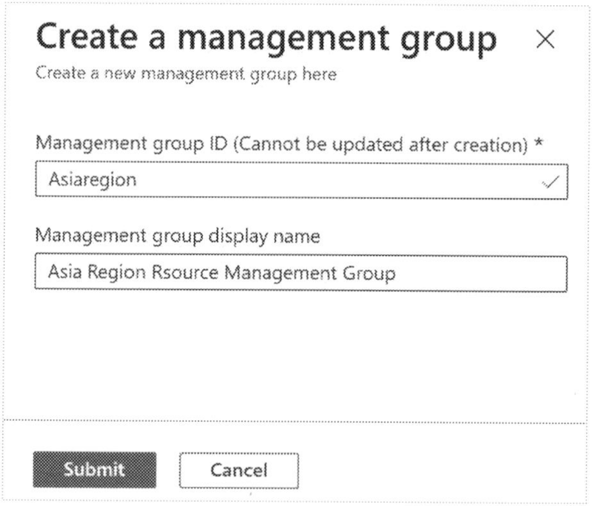

Create a management group ✕

Create a new management group here

Management group ID (Cannot be updated after creation) *

Asiaregion ✓

Management group display name

Asia Region Rsource Management Group

Submit   Cancel

Figure 2-3. *Creating management group*

Provide a management group id, which is required to identify the management group uniquely. Keep in mind that you need to select proper ID, because it cannot be updated after creation. Provide a proper name for the management group and click on the Submit button to create the new management group.

Azure has one management group by default as a root management group, so all the new resources will be added under the root group. You will be able to find the newly created management group if it is added as child group of the root group.

Your organization might require adding more Azure subscriptions. In this case, you can add subscriptions to the root management group by using the add subscription button in the management group overview page, as shown in Figure 2-4.

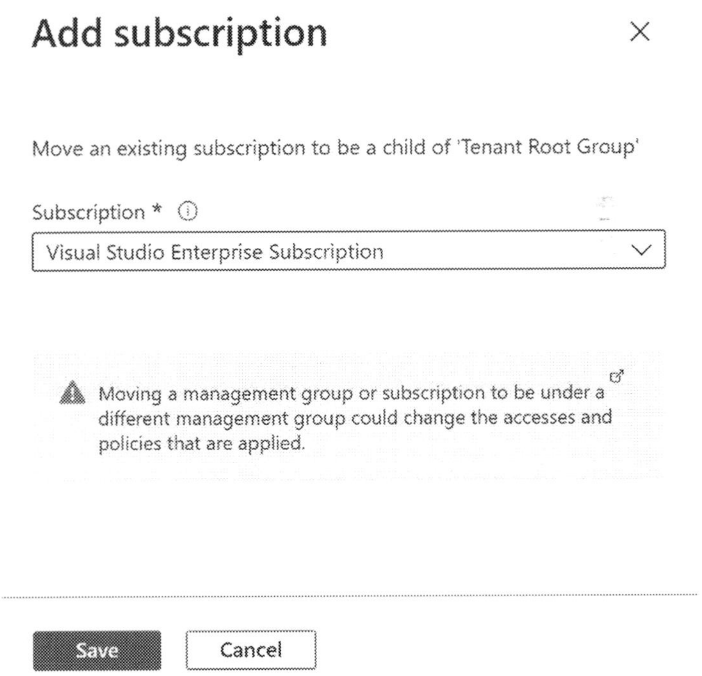

Add subscription   ✕

Move an existing subscription to be a child of 'Tenant Root Group'

Subscription * ⓘ

| Visual Studio Enterprise Subscription   ⌄ |

⚠ Moving a management group or subscription to be under a ⬀
different management group could change the accesses and
policies that are applied.

[Save]   [Cancel]

Figure 2-4. *Adding a subscription*

If you want to organize your management groups differently, go to the settings section of the management group and change the root group. You can also control the Azure Active Directory permission to create new management groups from this settings page (see Figure 2-5).

Figure 2-5. *Management group settings*

Now you know how to create a new management group and add subscriptions to the management group. Let's learn how we can control the security of the resources using a management group.

Click on a management group and go to the overview of the management group. You will be able to find the policy under the governance section (see Figure 2-6).

Figure 2-6. *Management group governance*

You can assign policies to the selected management group and it will be applied to the resources under the group, allowing you to organize your resources and manage security of the resources. You will be able to learn more about policies in the third section of this chapter.

In this lesson we have discussed the Azure subscriptions and management groups to identify the importance and usage.

Lesson 2.2: Azure Management Locks

Organizations can move the resources from on-premise to Azure cloud; however, merely moving your resources to Azure will not guarantee the application and data security. You need to introduce proper security measures to ensure the protection of application and data from various threats in the cloud more than you do in an on-premise environment. As you learned in the previous lesson, you can use several policies to protect and control the data in Azure. Other than the management groups, Azure has several other options to protect data. Azure management lock is one feature available in Azure that helps to improve the resource security.

As an Azure administrator, you can add locks to your Azure resources. You can add them in several levels. Azure management locks can be added to resource groups or individual resources. If you add Azure management lock to the resource group, that resource group cannot be deleted by another user who doesn't have permission. There are two types of locks available in Azure: ReadOnly lock and CanNotDelete.

ReadOnly grantsread-only permission to authorized users, meaning that they cannot delete or update the resource.

CanNotDelete means that authorized users with this permission can read and modify the resource, but cannot delete it.

You might be wondering how an organization benefits from applying Azure management locks.

Organizations use Azure platform to maintain and manage development environments as well as production environments. Organizations might have projects that have configured hundreds or thousands of resources in Azure cloud platform. They also might have spent months or years configuring those platforms, and numerous hours worth of employee work has been done. If a user accidently (or willingly with malicious intent) deletes such resources, it would be a huge loss for an organization and they would need to invest a lot of time and money to set up all the resources again. The organization could lose clients and the reputation of the company could be damaged. Resource lock may seem to be a minor feature, but you can add big value to the security of your Azure resources by enabling locks.

Now you know what resource lock is and the importance of it. Let's learn how to apply a resource lock to your resource.

First you need to identify where to put locks and in which situations to use them. If you fail to identify the requirements correctly, your resources will become unmanageable.

If you use Azure DevOps pipelines to deploy your resources via infrastructure as code tools, such as Terraform or Bicep, you need to give correct permission to service connection. Otherwise, if you apply resource locks via such infra scripts, you will not get the lock applied and may not even be able to modify a resource with a delete lock. Note that if you are thinking of adding locks for SQL server with the purpose of protecting the data in the SQL server, this purpose is not addressed with this feature. Locks only protect resources, not the data or functionalities related to the data. Likewise, you need to identify the security risk and apply the lock accordingly.

Let's learn how to apply a lock to a resource.

Go to Azure portal(`https://portal.azure.com/`) as an administrator, and select the resource that needs to be locked. Resource group is used in this example.

Click on the Locks of setting blade.

Click on the add button to add a new lock.

Provide a name for the lock and select lock type. You can add note to make sure what the lock really does. Click on OK (see Figure 2-7).

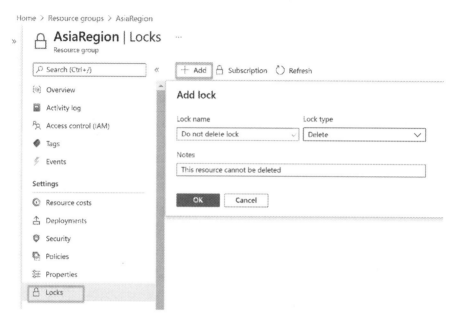

Figure 2-7. *Adding a lock*

Now you have added a lock to your resource.

If a user without permission accesses the lock, it will be shown as disabled (see Figure 2-8).

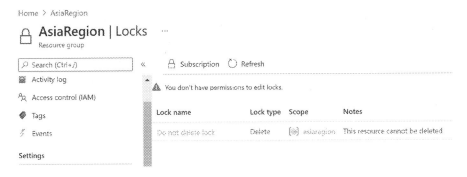

Figure 2-8. Locks

Only permitted users can delete or modify the resource, which gives protection from unnecessary actions performed on the resources either on purpose or mistakenly.

We have discussed the use of Azure resource locks to enhance security in this lesson.

Lesson 2.3: Introduction to Azure Policies

Policies are generally a set of rules and practices set to achieve a specific goal. In Azure, you can find policies that are used to achieve several requirements such as resource consistency, cost, management, regulatory compliance, and security. You will be able to learn how to use Azure policies to achieve an organization's security requirements in this lesson.

Azure policy has few components.

Business rules, also known as policy definition: This is a json file that has the logics used to check the resource compliant. This json file has two main components: meta data and rules. You are free to use functions, logical operations, parameters, conditions, and property aliases to build up the rules to meet the required scenarios.

Policy initiative: This can be identified as grouping of policy definitions for the purpose of management.

Once you set up a policy definition or policy initiative, you can assign it to resources such as management groups, subscriptions, resource groups, or individual resources. Properties of resources are then compared with policies and compliance is evaluated, as explained in the rules.

Now you know the basic concept behind the Azure policies. Next, you will learn when to assign policies and how to use them. See the policy evaluation flow example in Figure 2-9.

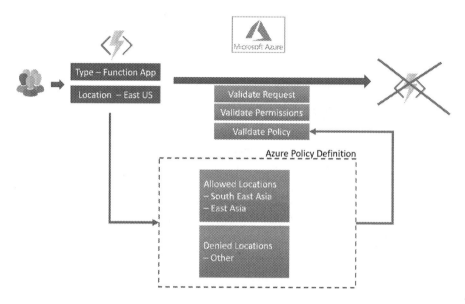

Figure 2-9. *Policy validation flow*

You can use these policies to set several security conditions to your resources. Organizations need to consider several data protection laws defined by respective governments. As an example, organizations situated in certain regions might have to obey data protection laws of governments demanding that they store data physically within a given region. Likewise, data in the European region can only be accessed or stored by users within that region. You can use Azure policies to configure such requirements.

You also need to understand the scope of the policy, which means that you need to know the resource level the policy is being applied to.

The broadest scope to which you can apply policy is management group, which might comprise of single or multiple subscriptions. Policy can be applied to multiple subscriptions by selecting the management group as the scope, and you can apply specific policies to each subscription. If you want a smaller scope than subscription level, you can apply policies to resource groups as well.

Let's learn how to add a new policy.

Go to `https://portal.azure.com/` and log in as an administrator. Search for policy (see Figure 2-10).

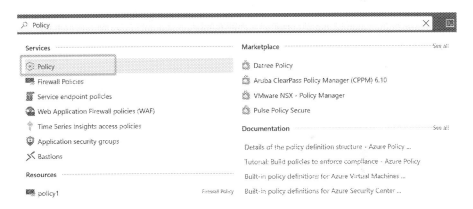

Figure 2-10. *Searching policy*

Click on the policy in the search result. The policy overview page will be opened.

Click on the definition under authoring. You will be able to see the new policy definition and initiative definition button, along with a list of predefined policies (see Figure 2-11). You can click on policy definition and add a new policy, or you can select existing policy from the list and apply it to the scope you want.

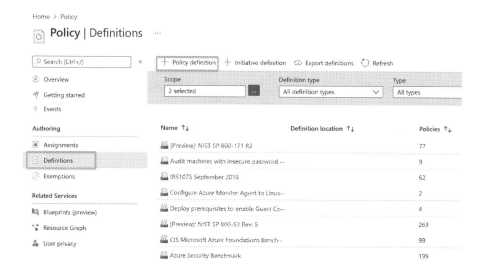

Figure 2-11. *Policy definitions*

First let's see how to add a new policy definition. Click on the policy definition, which will navigate you to the policy creation page (see Figure 2-12).

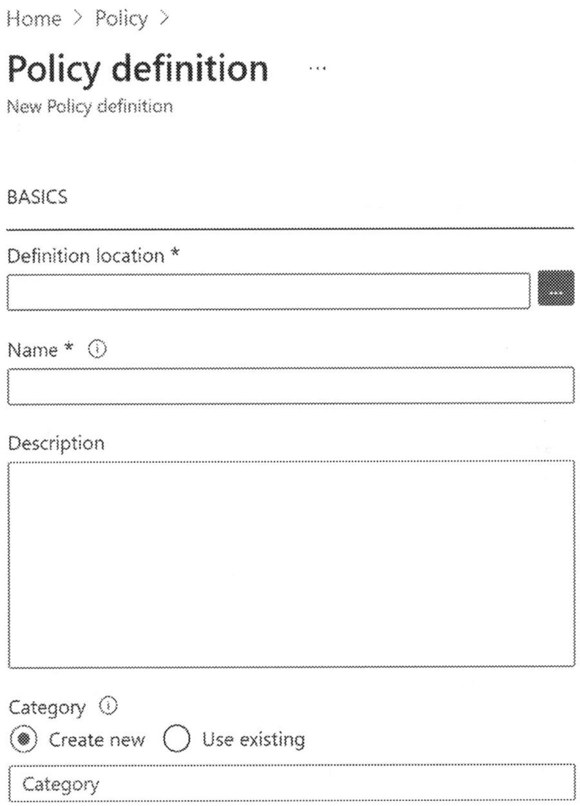

Home > Policy >

Policy definition   ...

New Policy definition

BASICS

Definition location *

Name * ⓘ

Description

Category ⓘ
⦿ Create new ◯ Use existing

Category

Figure 2-12. *Policy creation*

Definition location: Click on the three dot Infront of the definition location. It will open a pane where you can select the scope (see Figure 2-13).

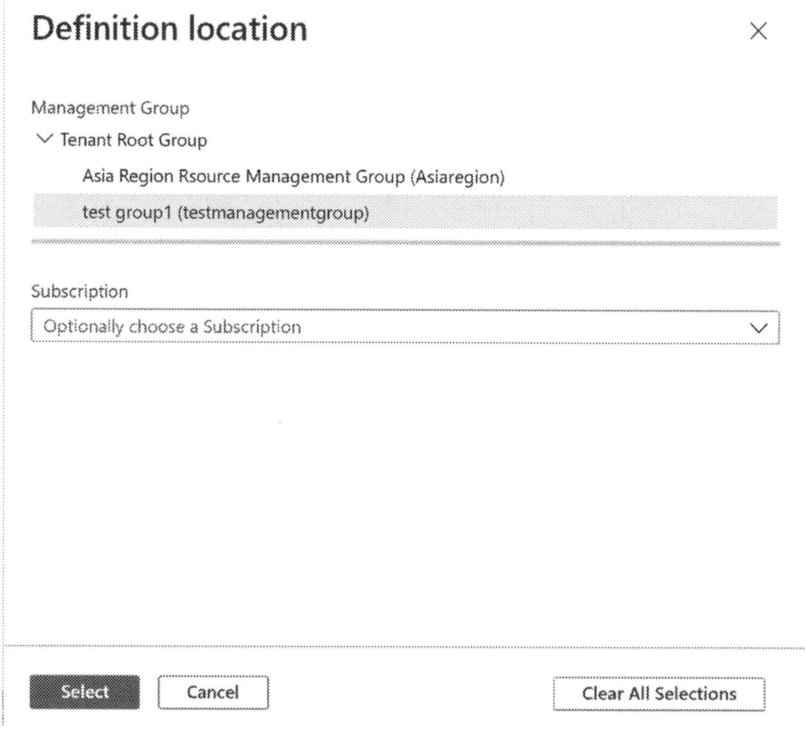

Definition location   ✕

Management Group

∨ Tenant Root Group

    Asia Region Rsource Management Group (Asiaregion)

    test group1 (testmanagementgroup)

Subscription

| Optionally choose a Subscription ∨ |

| Select | Cancel | | Clear All Selections |

***Figure 2-13.** Definition location*

Name: Provide a name for the policy.

Description: Here you can provide a detailed description about the policy.

Category: Select the category in which your policy is being applied. As an example, your policy can be related to KeyVault, App services, or any other resources. You have options to create a new category, or you can select an existing category for the policy from this feature.

Policy rule: You can write a Json file that has the conditions you want to fulfil using the policy (see Figure 2-14).

Figure 2-14. *Policy rule*

Finally, you can save the details and create a custom policy to apply to your Azure resources.

You have learned how to create a custom policy. Let's see how to apply the policy to a selected scope.

Select the policy from the list. You can select filters at the top of the page to search for the required policies (see Figure 2-15).

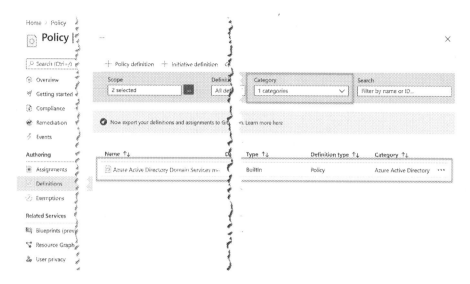

Figure 2-15. *Filtering a policy*

Click on the selected policy. It will open the page where you can see the policy rules. Click on the assign button to assign the selected policy to the resource (see Figure 2-16).

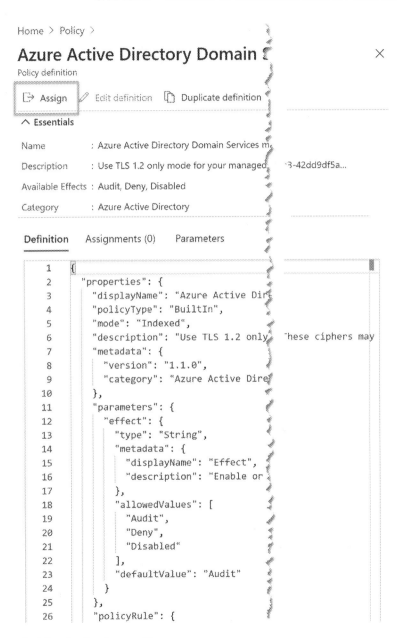

Figure 2-16. *Assigning policy*

You will be able to see the page where you can select scope to assign a policy (see Figure 2-17).

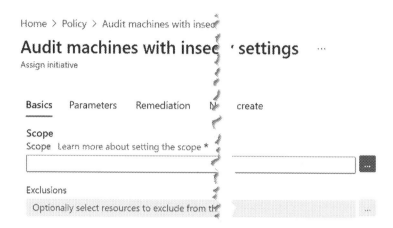

Figure 2-17. *Assigning policy window*

Click on three dot Infront of the scope textbox. It will open the pane where you can select the scope of the policy (see Figure 2-18).

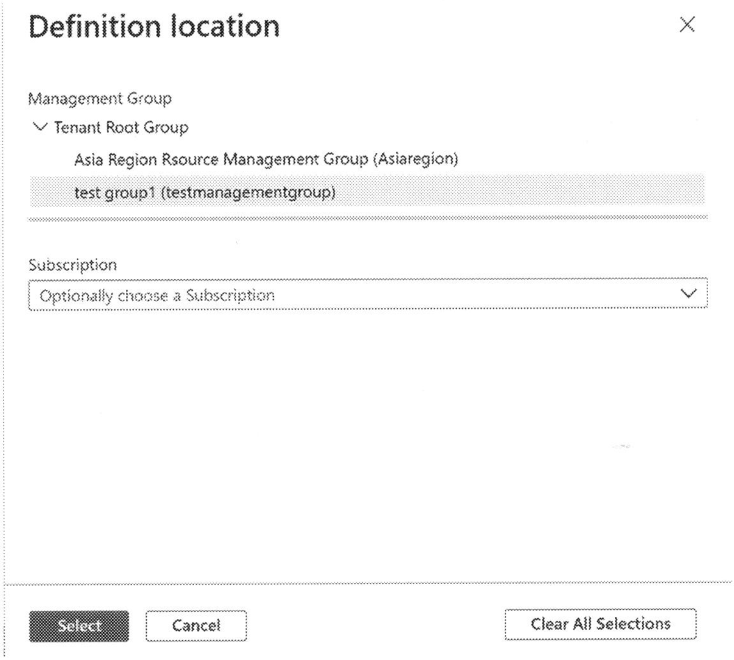

Figure 2-18. Assigning policy scope

Exclusions: There can be some resources you do not want to apply the policy. Azure has the feature to exclude the resources from policy.

Click on the three dots in front of Exclusions (see Figure 2-17). A pane will open where you can select the resource to exclude (see Figure 2-19).

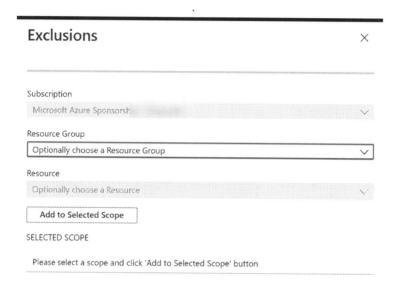

Figure 2-19. *Exclusions*

Policy enforcement: Using policy enforcement, you can define the enforcement to be enabled so the policy will be actively checking any new resources created or any resource updated for policy adherence. Disabling policy enforcement will let you check the "what if" state if the policy is applied in other words, you can preview how the policy will be affecting resources (see Figure 2-20).

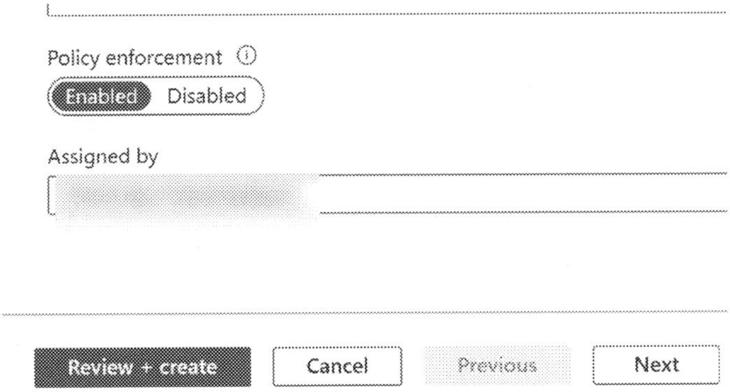

Figure 2-20. *Policy enforcement*

Depending on the selected policy, you might have to set different parameters for it. For example, the CORS policy for function app has an Effect parameter that allows Audit or Disabled to be used as values (see Figure 2-21). Such parameters will be based on the definition in the policy rules.

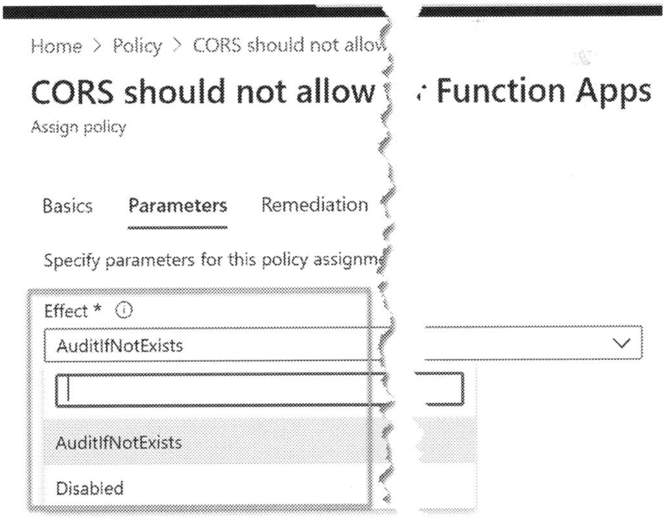

Figure 2-21. *Parameters*

Depending on the policy, setting up remediation action can be assigned to be performed in situations where policy is violated. For example, Figure 2-22 shows a remediation action of creating a managed identity.

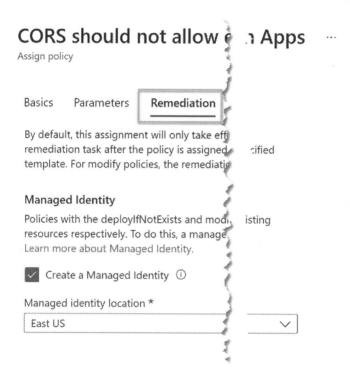

Figure 2-22. Remediation

It is even possible to set up a custom compliance message when assigning a policy. You can assign the policy to resources following the wizard and evaluate your resource for compliance.

In this lesson we have discussed how policies can be defined to enhance security in Azure resources.

Summary

In this chapter, we have focused on identifying Azure subscriptions and management groups. Then we explored the ability to use resource locks and policies to enable security in Azure resources.

Let's explore Azure active directory related security configurations in the next chapter.

CHAPTER 3

Introduction to Azure Active Directory

Controlling access management of the resources is an important part of the security configurations. When you provide access to the resources, you need to decide who gets which level of access. Azure active directory facilitates these particular access management needs.

Azure active directory is a service that helps to control employee (user) identity and access management for the applications and data of your organization or external resources.

Lesson 3.1: Adding Users and Groups to the AD

The main functionality of AAD (Azure Active Directory) is identity and access management. Adding users to AAD and grouping them according to the permission levels is the basic use of AAD.

Go to `https://portal.azure.com` and log in as the admin user of Azure subscription.

Search for Azure Active Directory, and it will appear in the search results (see Figure 3-1).

© Pushpa Herath 2022
P. Herath, *Azure Cloud Security for Absolute Beginners*,
https://doi.org/10.1007/978-1-4842-7860-4_3

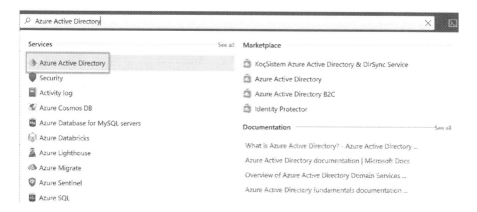

Figure 3-1. *Searching for AAD*

Next, open Azure Active Directory.

Select users from the side setting blade (see Figure 3-2).

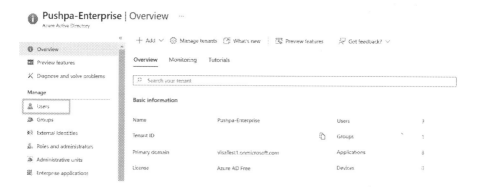

Figure 3-2. *Users*

Click on the users and it will open the users overview page. You can add new users or invite guest users to access your organization resources (see Figure 3-3). When you add new users, there are options to select the permission level each user may be assigned.

Figure 3-3. *New user*

Click on create new user to add new user to your organization. These users can have various permission levels.

Having several levels of permissions enables the freedom to decide who has which permission, and permission can be controlled to secure the applications and data while also ensuring that users have enough access to perform the required work.

In addition to adding new users to your AAD, you can invite users as guests to join your AAD to obtain access to the resources in your Azure subscriptions.

You can also create groups and add multiple users or groups as members to the group to control the permission for multiple users at once (see Figure 3-4). This will enable more organized access management and will make maintenance of access management simple and easy.

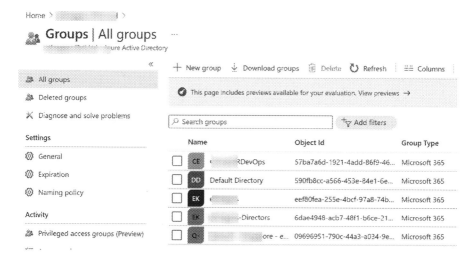

Figure 3-4. *Groups*

In this lesson, we discussed creating Azure Active Directory (AAD) users and groups to manage access control.

Lesson 3.2: Managing External Identities

Azure Active directory has the capability to organize and manage the customers and partners of your organization who are recognized as external identities. It helps to interact and share resources and applications with external parties securely. The Azure AD external identities feature allows external users outside of your organization to access your apps using their preferred identities.

There are two types of external identity management techniques in Azure AD: B2B (Business to Business) and B2C (Business to Consumer).

Business to Business (B2B)

In the business world, companies do collaborative work if there is such a requirement in the market. These can be outsourced consultants or partners. But companies need to protect their business plans and secrets while working collaboratively with external parties. The Azure B2B identity management feature can be used to achieve this.

You can add external users to your organization's AAD and can securely share your organization's application and services with the guest users without revealing any of your corporate data. Guest users can also use their own credentials to access your organization's applications and services.

You can easily send an invitation to a guest user, and the user will be added to AAD along with other users (see Figure 3-5).

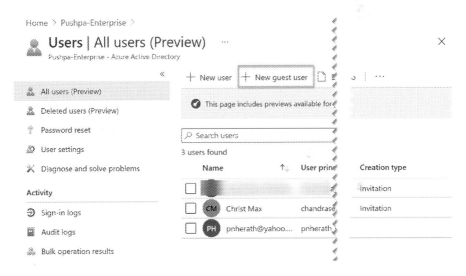

Figure 3-5. *Inviting guest user*

Click on New guest user, as shown in Figure 3-5. Add required details of the guest user and send an invitation. Guest users will receive an email with the invitation. Once the invitation is accepted, guest users can access allowed applications and services.

Additionally, you can add external identity providers to allow guest user access. Once external identity providers are federated with your Azure

AD, your external users can use their own social or corporate accounts to sign into your applications.

Let's see how to integrate such authentication services with Azure AD.

Go to Azure portal and log in as an administrator, then go to Azure Active directory and select external identities from the side setting, as shown in Figure 3-6.

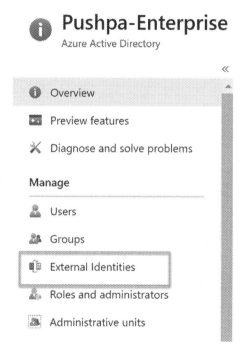

Figure 3-6. *External identities*

Select all identity providers, and you will be able to see available identity provider options (see Figure 3-7).

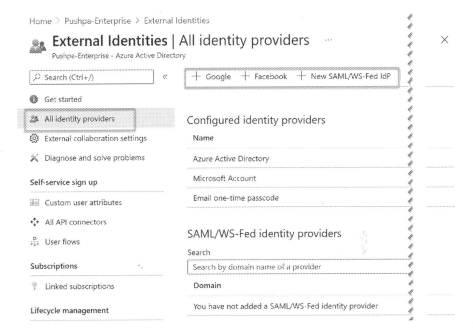

Figure 3-7. *Adding external identity provider*

You may need to create a client ID and a secret based on the external identity service you are configuring, and provide them in Azure AD to create the connectivity (see Figure 3-8).

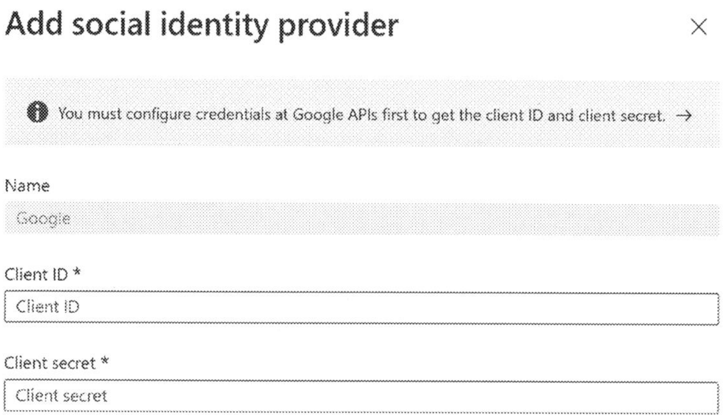

Add social identity provider   ✕

ℹ You must configure credentials at Google APIs first to get the client ID and client secret. →

Name

Google

Client ID *

Client ID

Client secret *

Client secret

Figure 3-8. *Configuring Google as provider*

Once you enable the external identity providers you will be able to
configure applications to use external identity providers.

Business to consumer (B2C)

Azure AD B2C allows you to customize how your users sign up, sign in,
or manage their profiles when using your applications. The first item you
need to set up is Azure AD B2C tenant. Azure AD B2C tenant is a collection
of identities to be used with applications relying on the B2C tenant,
whereas Azure AD tenants represent an organization.

Azure AD B2C directory lets you keep users' credentials, profile data,
and application registrations. Application registrations can be your APIs,
web, or mobile applications. You can define custom user flows, and
custom policies can be used to build complex identity flows. Azure AD B2C
allows various types of sign-in options such as user name, password, use
of social media identity providers, and use of external identity providers
federated with protocols such as OAuth 2 and open ID connect (OIDC)
(see Figure 3-9).

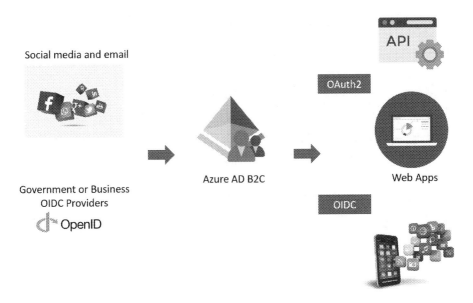

Figure 3-9. Azure AD B2C

It is also possible to manage the encryption keys required to sign in with tokens, passwords, certificates, and client secrets. Similar to Azure AD tenant, a B2C tenant also has several types of accounts. Users with work accounts are allowed to access and manage Azure resources based on the assigned roles. Guest or external account users can also manage Azure resources based on given roles. However, consumer accounts created in a B2C tenant only lets users sign in and use the applications secured with the B2C tenant. These consumer account users cannot access Azure resources. They are the B2C users who are experiencing the custom sign-up and sign-in workflows in your application as defined in B2C tenant policies and user flows.

We have discussed Azure AD B2B and B2C setup and its usage in this lesson.

Lesson 3.3: Enabling Multifactor Authentications

Organizations need to manage the identities of the users to secure the data and resources owned by the organization as well as their customers. Identity management is the mechanism used to control unauthorized access to the organization's resources. However, with the development of technologies, bypassing a password and accessing resources without permission is possible. As a solution to that, multifactor authentications (MFAs) are introduced that add an extra layer of security for your resources.

Let's understand what can be identified as multifactor authentications.

Multifactor authentication has more than one authentication mechanism as an extra layer of security. As an example, you can have a password or pin along with verification done via random code generated, authenticated via mobile application or SMS. You can also use face recognition or fingerprints as additional authentication mechanisms.

Any combination of two of three mechanisms can be identified as multifactor authentication:

- Password or pin, which is added while creating identity

- Fingerprint or facial recognition unique to a user

- Phone or devices that can be used for verifications

Now you understand multifactor authentication, but why do you need to it, and why is it not possible to add enough security by having a single password?

There are several reasons to add multifactor authentications. With modern technicalogical development and the connected nature of the world, people are using numerous web services including online shopping, Internet banking, and social media accounts. The risky part of using many web services is in reusing the same password or PIN in several sites, which is due to the human nature of keeping things simple. If someone finds your password in one location, they might be able to access all of your accounts and other important services that can harm you financially and affect your social image as well. If you use your organization account in a third-party service, your user credentials will be saved in their servers and external parties can access the organizational data and systems, which add a huge risk to your organization.

Phishing attacks are another kind of security threat possible when using one password. Phishing occurs when you receive an email asking you to verify your user name and password. Without understanding the risk involved, many users reveal their username and password to attackers this way. If you have used only a username and password as authentication mechanism, an attacker can easily access all your important Internet services. However, if you have configured your mobile phone as a second layer of authentication, an attacker cannot log in to your accounts without having access to your mobile phone.

Another risk is having weak passwords that can be easily decoded by hackers. Password standards are used to reduce the risk of having predictable weak passwords, but again it is not enough to secure your organization's resources.

There are several versions of MFAs available with Azure, such as those provided with Office 365, which requires users to authenticate in each sign-in. There is another version of MFA that allows Azure active directory global administrator users to have two-step authentications without any additional cost for the service. Azure Active directory global administrators have the topmost authority to Azure active directory, which is mandatory to have as much security as possible. Azure multifactor authentication is another version of MFA that allows users to have a specific set of defined permissions.

You have learned how to add new users to the Azure active directory in the previous section of this chapter. Let's now learn how to add user MFA.

Go to https://portal.azure.com/ and log in as an administrator, then go to the active directory and select users. This will open the all user page.

You will be able to see per-user MFA button available (see Figure 3-10).

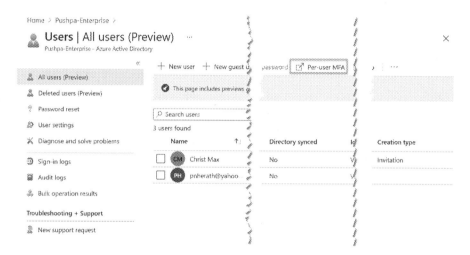

Figure 3-10. *Per user MFA*

Click on the per-user MFA button. You will be navigated to the multifactor authentication page (see Figure 3-11).

multi-factor authentication
users service settings
View: Sign-in allowed users
bulk update
DISPLAY NAME
USER NAME
MULTI-FACTOR AUTH STATUS
Christ Max
Disabled
pnherath@yahoo.com herath
Disabled
quick steps
Enable
Manage user settings

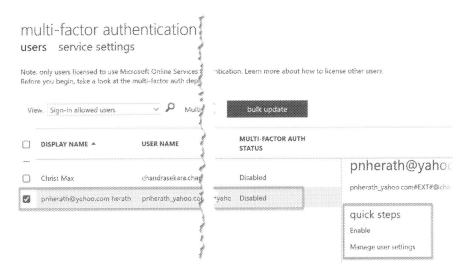

Figure 3-11. *MFA page*

Select the user from the list and click on Enable to enable multifactor authentication (see Figure 3-12).

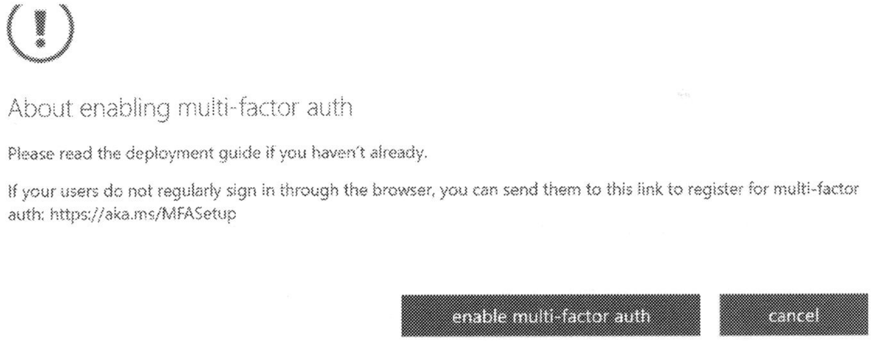

About enabling multi-factor auth
Please read the deployment guide if you haven't already.
If your users do not regularly sign in through the browser, you can send them to this link to register for multi-factor auth: https://aka.ms/MFASetup
enable multi-factor auth
cancel

Figure 3-12. *Enabling MFA*

We have discussed multifactor authentication and explored how to enable MFA for a user in Azure AD.

Lesson 3.4: Roles and Administrative Units in Azure AD

Azure active directory has the ability to apply several user permissions to secure the organizational data and applications. Organizations can assign user access only for the relevant areas or resources. However, you should use these access permission features intelligently to apply an effective security strategy. If this is not done, you will not be able to get the full use of the features.

Your organization might be a large one that shares one tenant across multiple subscriptions. However, you might need to divide your resources into several sections because of business requirements. As an example, you might have grouped your business as multiple business units. If you have two business units, such as as marketing and engineering, administrators of marketing should not have permission to control engineering business unit users, groups, or permission and engineering administrators should not have the ability to control marketing users, groups, and permissions. Such control is required to avoid security vulnerability to your organization due to unnecessary permissions.

You need a mechanism to give each unit the ability to manage only its own features. You can use administrative units to solve this security vulnerability in your organization.

Go to `https://portal.azure.com/` and log in as an administrator.

Next, open Azure Active Directory.

Select Administrative units and click on Add button to add a new administrative unit (see Figure 3-13).

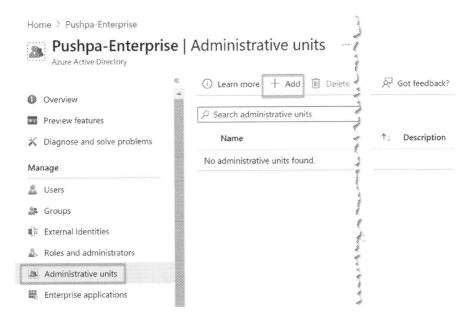

Figure 3-13. *Administrative units*

Add name and description for the administrative unit (see
Figure 3-14).

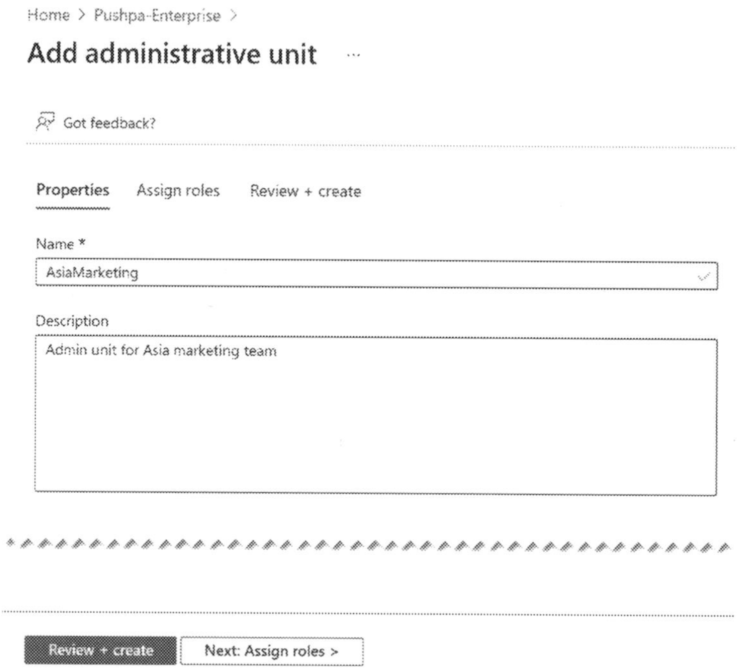

Home > Pushpa-Enterprise >

Add administrative unit   ···

💬 Got feedback?

Properties   Assign roles   Review + create

Name *

| AsiaMarketing |

Description

| Admin unit for Asia marketing team |

[Review + create]   [Next: Assign roles >]

Figure 3-14. *Adding administrative unit*

Once filled, basic information moves to the Assign roles section.
You can select the administrative role that you are going to use with the
unit. There are several roles. User administrator role, which is allowed
to manage all aspects of users and groups, including reset password for
limited admins which is selected in this sample (see Figure 3-15).

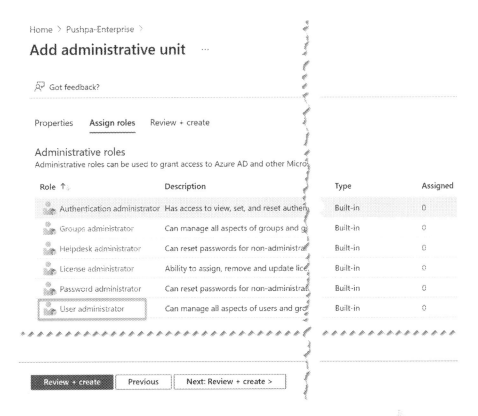

Figure 3-15. *Assigning roles*

Click on the role and you will be able to search for existing users and assign roles to selected users (see Figure 3-16). Note that to assign users or groups to roles, you must have an Azure AD p1 or P2 premium licence.

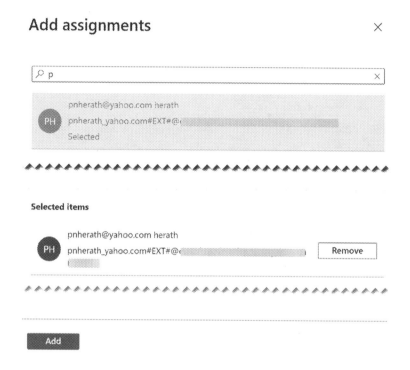

Figure 3-16. *Adding users to role*

Selected users will be assigned for the selected role. Go to Review and create a page and verify the values entered. If you are happy with the configuration, click on the create button to add a new administrative unit.

Click on the newly created administrative unit. You will be able to add users and groups, and manage or change roles of the administrative unit (see Figure 3-17).

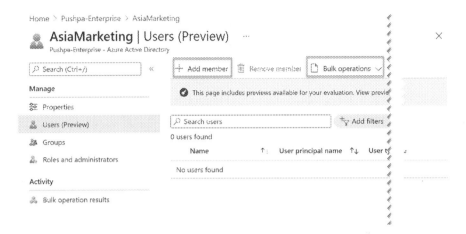

Figure 3-17. *Users in administrative unit*

You can click on Add members to add new members to this administrative unit, as shown in Figure 3-17. You can add members individually, or you can add members as bulk using the bulk operations section. As depicted in Figure 3-18, an administrative unit will have one or more admins (who can be assigned to administrative unit roles if you have P1 or P2 premium AD), and they can manage added users or groups to the administrative unit.

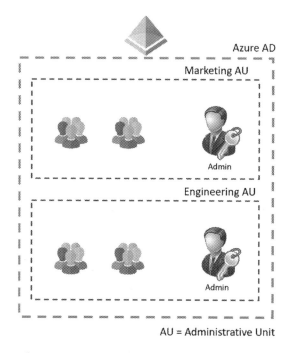

Figure 3-18. *Administrative unit example*

This section has discussed the usage and steps to create administrative units in Azure AD to have required isolation in permission management.

Lesson 3.5: Managing Applications

There are two types of applications involved with Azure AD. The first is application registration, which is a way of setting up your application URL with Azure AD so that it can communicate with your AD and enable hooking up with Azure AD services. Enterprise applications, on the other hand, refers to external applications published in Azure AD gallery, where you can utilize them within your organization.

Managing Enterprise Applications

Organizations use various enterprise applications to fulfill their business needs. Those tools can be applications that cater to several services such as continuous integration and deployment, team collaboration, and cloud platforms. If those external enterprise applications need to be used within the organization, you can integrate those enterprise applications in Azure Active Directory.

Go to `https://portal.azure.com/`.and log in as an administrator, then go to Azure Active directory.

Select Enterprise applications to find the enterprise applications you can integrate with Azure Active Directory. Click on a new application to add a new enterprise application (see Figure 3-19).

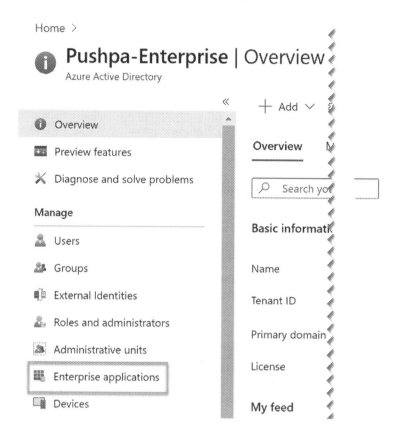

Figure 3-19. *Enterprise applications*

You will be able to see several enterprise applications that can be integrated. Select an application that you need to integrate to your AD (see Figure 3-20).

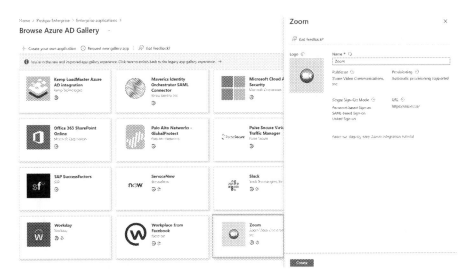

Figure 3-20. *Azure AD gallery*

You can open a newly added application page and apply the required configurations, such as single sign-in.

Azure AD App Registration

App registration is the definition of the application that includes various application elements such as URI, name, secrets, and more. It can be identified as an object in Azure AD that describes the application. App registration enables communication between Azure and applications and passes tokens to the application. You can integrate applications you develop to Azure via the app registration feature of Azure AD.

If you integrate your app with Azure, Azure AD assigns a unique application ID and provides several services, such as permission and role management and sign-ins.

Go to `https://portal.azure.com/` and log in as an administrator.

Go to Azure Active directory.

Click on App registration. You will be able to see all the available app registrations. If you want to get client ID and more data of app registration, you need to click on the relevant app registration name from the list (see Figure 3-21).

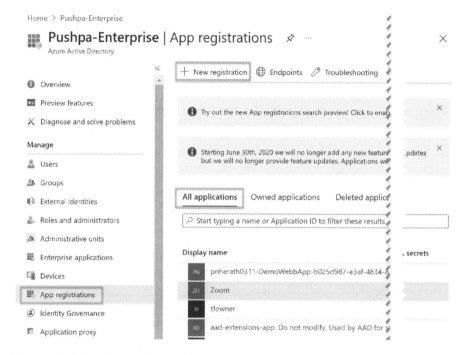

Figure 3-21. *App registrations*

If you need to create a new app registration, click on the New registration button. It will open a page where you can create the app registration (see Figure 3-22).

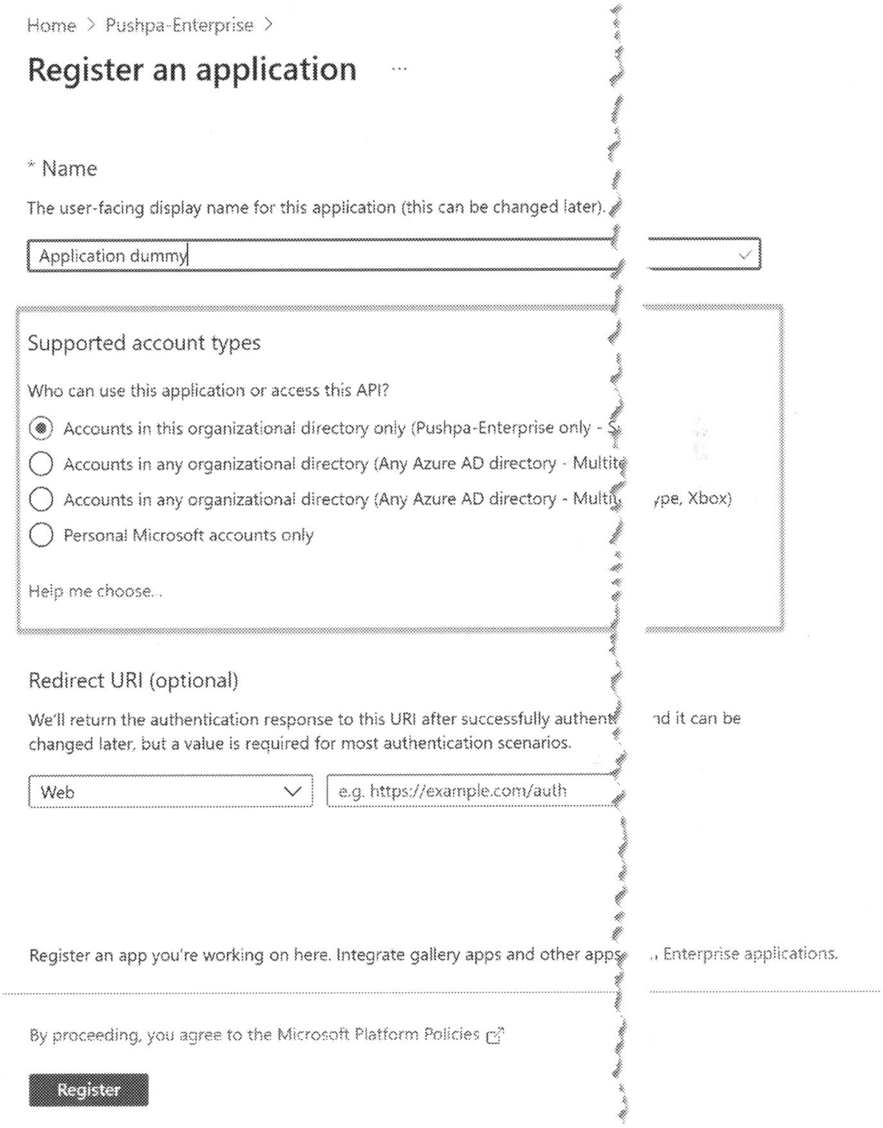

Home > Pushpa-Enterprise >

Register an application   ...

* Name

The user-facing display name for this application (this can be changed later).

Application dummy

Supported account types

Who can use this application or access this API?

(●) Accounts in this organizational directory only (Pushpa-Enterprise only - S

( ) Accounts in any organizational directory (Any Azure AD directory - Multite

( ) Accounts in any organizational directory (Any Azure AD directory - Multi   ype, Xbox)

( ) Personal Microsoft accounts only

Help me choose...

Redirect URI (optional)

We'll return the authentication response to this URI after successfully authent   nd it can be
changed later, but a value is required for most authentication scenarios.

| Web | ⌄ | e.g. https://example.com/auth |

Register an app you're working on here. Integrate gallery apps and other apps   ., Enterprise applications.

By proceeding, you agree to the Microsoft Platform Policies ⌕

Register

Figure 3-22. *Creating app registration*

You can provide a display name for the app registration, account
type, which decides who can use this application or access the API. Click
on register to add application. Once it is added, you can control

authentication, certificate, secrets, and more security components related to your application.

In this lesson we have explored enterprise applications and app registrations in Azure.

Lesson 3.6: Introduction to AD Devices

Organizations use several applications to cater to their organizational needs. There are applications such as Office 365, that are protected by Azure active directory. Users mainly access these applications from inside the organization's network via organization-provided devices.

If you consider the devices provided by the organization, those are domain joined devices. By doing that, it makes a connection between your device and active directory device management. Your active directory device management can be used to manage the identity of the domain joined devices.

You might have only Azure AD as your domain server, and in such situations your devices are joined to Azure AD (see Figure 3-23).

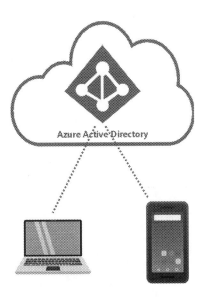

Figure 3-23. *AAD joined devices*

If you have on-premises Active directory that is in sync with Azure AD, your devices can sync with both using Azure active directory connect (see Figure 3-24).

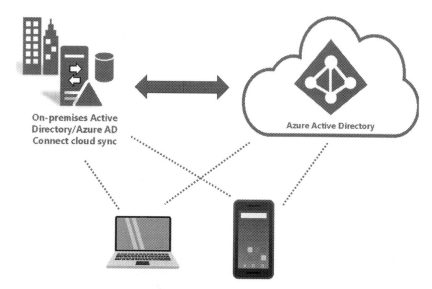

Figure 3-24. *AD and AAD sync*

Azure AD Registered versus Azure AD-Joined Devices

You can register any device running MacOS, iOS, or Android. However, to join a device to Azure AD, it needs to run a Windows-based operating system. Azure AD-joined devices demand that the user sign in to the device with the active directory account only (see Figure 3-25).

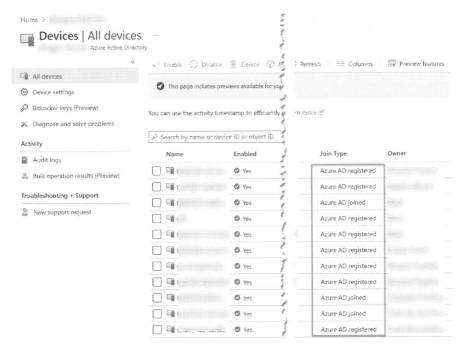

Figure 3-25. *AD registered versus joined*

Lesson 3.7: Adding Custom Domains

Organizations need to maintain a distinctive brand to remain competitive in the modern business world. Providing special services, quality work, and well-maintained reputation are a few of the important areas required for an organization to be successful.

In terms of the branding, the organization should have a proper domain name to build a trust with clients. This also strengthens the brand and drives traffic to the organization's site.

In addition to branding, it helps to win clients' trust by reducing the risk of phishing scams. If an organization is able to have a proper domain name, clients know your domain and they will click on the links on your Internet promotions without being a victim of phishing attacks.

Custom domain can add business value as well as security for your clients, which improves the trust on the business.

Azure Active directory has a feature where you can link a custom domain to your organization.

As a prerequisite, you need to purchase a custom domain name from a domain name provider service.

Go to `https://portal.azure.com/` and log in as an administrator.

Go to Azure Active directory. You will be able to find custom domain names setting in the side settings of AAD. Click on custom domain names and click on Add custom domain (see Figure 3-26).

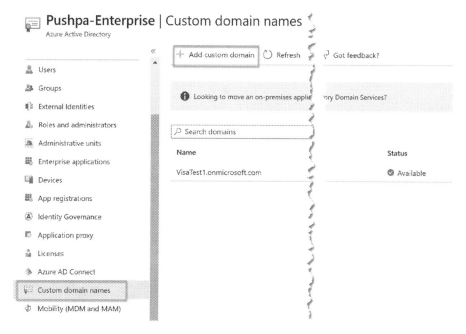

Figure 3-26. *Custom domains*

A side pane will be opened where you can enter the custom domain name. Add a custom domain name and click on Add domain button (see Figure 3-27).

Custom domain na...   ✕

Pushpa-Enterprise

Custom domain name * ⓘ

| VisaTest1.com | ✓ |

Add domain

Figure 3-27. *Adding domain*

After adding the custom domain, you need to verify that the domain
name is owned by you. TXT or MX values need to be added to the domain
name registry, and you need to verify it in Azure to confirm the ownership
of the domain. Once you have added the destination or point to address
for the domain name, click on the Verify button to verify the domain name
(see Figure 3-28).

Figure 3-28. Verifying domain

Once the verification is completed, the active directory will build a link with the domain name provider.

This lesson has demonstrated the steps to add a custom domain to Azure AD.

Summary

This chapter has explored user management in Azure AD, including external identities, enhancing security with multifactor authentication, and roles and administrative units to enable implementation of effective security strategy. We have also explored registering devices, managing applications, and assigning custom domains to Azure AD.

In the next chapter, let's explore how to work with Azure Key Vault.

CHAPTER 4

Working with Azure Key Vault

Technology has become part of our everyday lives, with the devices and services we use. Technological developments, global connectivity, and complex and advanced technical innovations are bringing the world to our fingertips in modern times. Internet banking and online shopping have become the norm now. Such a connected nature of modern applications demands high security of data and applications. It is essential to keep application secrets such as application connections to data, third-party service keys, certificates, and even underlying API URLs secure.

As secret management has an important role in applications, as a secret management solution, Azure offers a key vault. Azure key vault offers hardware encrypted security to all your secrets, keys, and certificates with a level of permission and access management as well as network security policies to ensure that your secrets are safer in public cloud environments.

Lesson 4.1: Setting Up Key Vault

Azure key vault is a cloud service that provides secure storage and access for keys, secrets, and certificates. It can be used to store passwords, certificates, and keys such as API keys. Key vault can also be used to generate passwords up to security standards. It helps users generate and

© Pushpa Herath 2022
P. Herath, *Azure Cloud Security for Absolute Beginners*,
https://doi.org/10.1007/978-1-4842-7860-4_4

maintain unique strong passwords for each Internet service they use
without using the same weak password everywhere.

Let's learn how to create an Azure key vault.

Go to https://portal.azure.com/ and log in as an administrator.

Search for the term Key vaults and select key vaults from the search
result (see Figure 4-1).

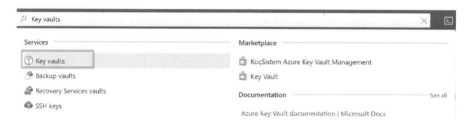

Figure 4-1. *Searching for key vault setting*

Click on the create button to start the creation process (see Figure 4-2).

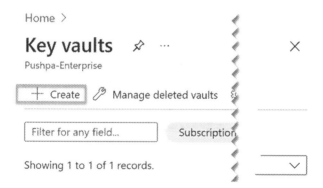

Figure 4-2. *Creating new key vault*

Enter required values for a key vault such as resource group, region,
key vault name, and pricing tier (see Figure 4-3).

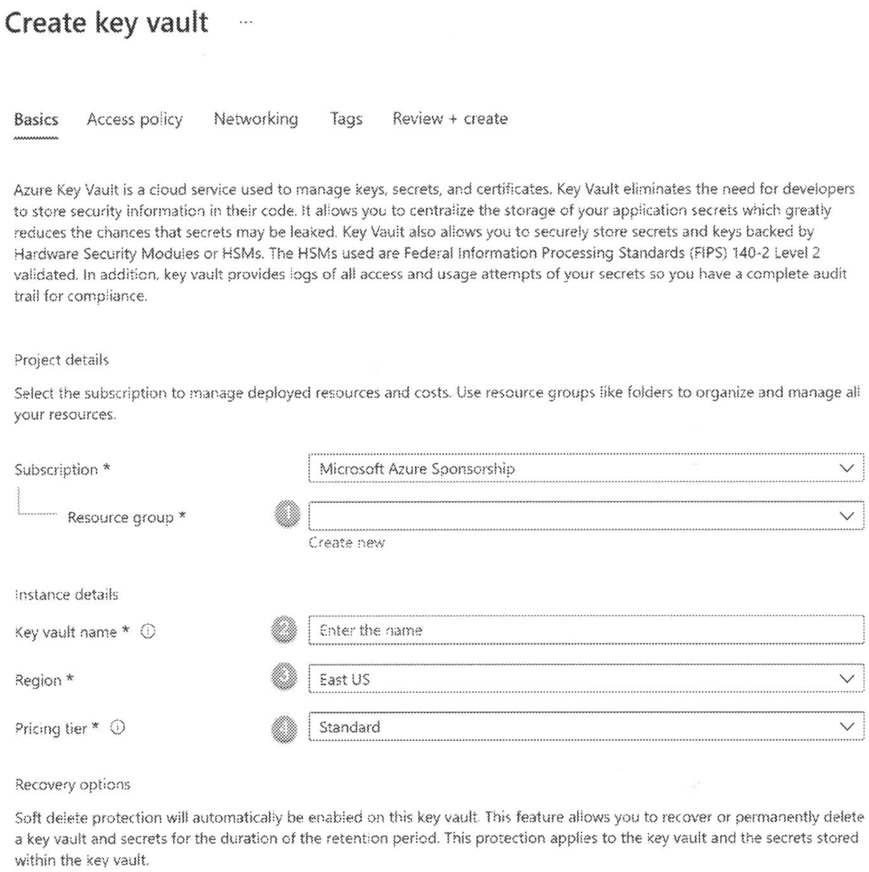

Create key vault   ...

Basics   Access policy   Networking   Tags   Review + create

Azure Key Vault is a cloud service used to manage keys, secrets, and certificates. Key Vault eliminates the need for developers to store security information in their code. It allows you to centralize the storage of your application secrets which greatly reduces the chances that secrets may be leaked. Key Vault also allows you to securely store secrets and keys backed by Hardware Security Modules or HSMs. The HSMs used are Federal Information Processing Standards (FIPS) 140-2 Level 2 validated. In addition, key vault provides logs of all access and usage attempts of your secrets so you have a complete audit trail for compliance.

Project details

Select the subscription to manage deployed resources and costs. Use resource groups like folders to organize and manage all your resources.

Subscription * | Microsoft Azure Sponsorship   ⌄ |

    ⌐ Resource group *   ① | ⌄ |
                                  Create new

Instance details

Key vault name * ⓘ   ② | Enter the name |

Region *   ③ | East US   ⌄ |

Pricing tier * ⓘ   ④ | Standard   ⌄ |

Recovery options

Soft delete protection will automatically be enabled on this key vault. This feature allows you to recover or permanently delete a key vault and secrets for the duration of the retention period. This protection applies to the key vault and the secrets stored within the key vault.

Figure 4-3. *Key vault values*

1. Select existing resource group or new resource group. Once the key vault creation process is complete, you will be able to find your key vault inside this resource group.

2. Give the name for your key vault.

3. Select the region where you want to create the key vault.

4.   Select the pricing for the key vault. There are two
     options: Standard and Premium. The difference
     between these pricing tiers are that premium
     allows you to create (hardware security module
     (HSM)-protected keys, and standard does not have
     that option.

Next, you need to select recovery options (see Figure 4-4).

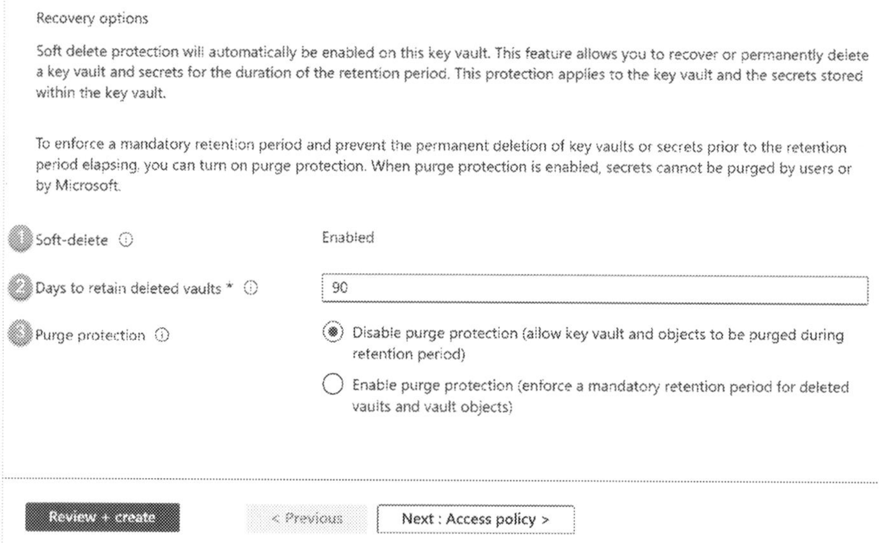

Figure 4-4. *Recovery options*

1.   Soft delete feature allows users to recover the
     deleted vaults and deleted keys, secrets, and
     certificates. Now it is mandatory to enable soft
     delete on any Azure key vault.

2.   Users can define the period for retaining the deleted
     vault. This value must be between seven and
     90 days.

3. Enable Purge protection is an irreversible action
    that you cannot change to disable once the key vault
    is created. However, if you choose not to enable
    protection at the creation time, you can enable it
    later. If the purge protection is not enabled, you can
    purge the deleted key vaults and key vault objects
    during the retention period.

If you enable purge protection, you have to wait for the entire retention period to purge the deleted key vaults and key vault objects.

You can add access policies and network configurations while creating a new key vault or after completing the creation process. You can learn more about access policies and networking in later lessons of this chapter.

Once all the required values are added, go to Review and create a section to make sure you have selected the correct configurations for the key vault. Finally, click on the Create button to create a key vault.

We have discussed why we need a key vault and how to create a key vault using an Azure portal in this lesson.

Lesson 4.2: Key Vault Access Control

Controlling access to a resource is an important concern of security. Azure key vault is a place where all the important passwords, secrets, and other keys are stored. Therefore, it is mandatory to secure a key vault by controlling the access.

Go to `https://portal.azure.com/` and log in as an administrator.

Go to Access Control and click on Add button to add role assignment, as shown in Figure 4-5. Once you click on Add button, you can see the options to add role assignment or add co administrator. Click on Add role assignment.

Figure 4-5. *Access control*

A side pane will be opened where you can enter required details for role assignment (see Figure 4-6).

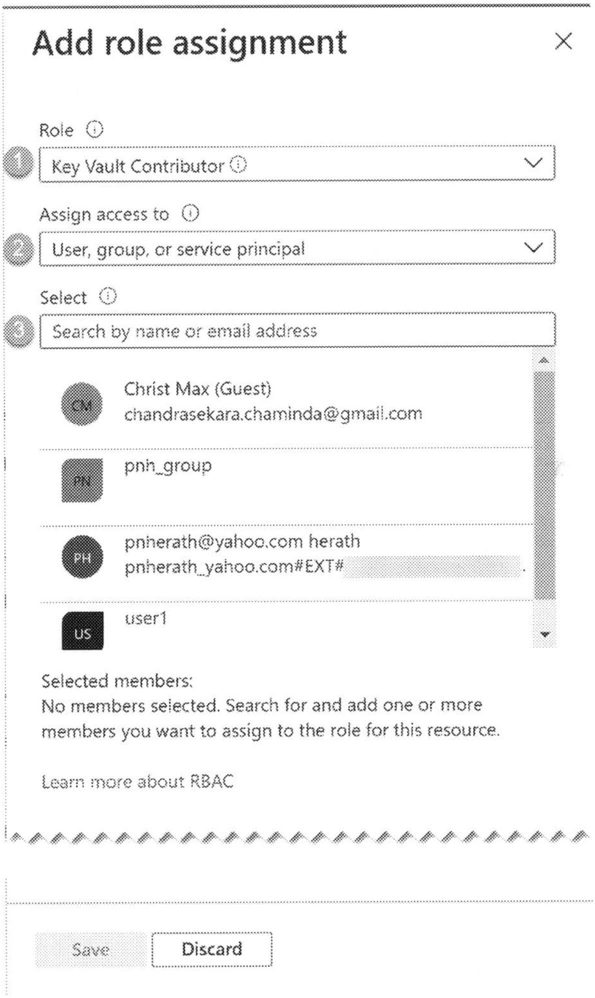

Figure 4-6. *Adding role assignment*

1. Select the role to assign. Each role has different capabilities. For example, you can use the contributor role in a scenario where you have to allow the user to manage the key vault in the management pane; however, this will prevent the user from accessing the key vault keys, secrets, and certificates.

2. Assign who or which Azure resource gets access to
    the key vault. There can be a specific user or user
    group that needs access to the key vault. If you keep
    application secret values in the key vault for app
    service or function apps, you can allow the function
    apps or app services access to the key vault. You
    can select the category for which you are going to
    provide access to the key vault from this drop down.

3. If you select App service as access category, you can
    select the relevant app service from the list. If you
    select users and groups, then you will be able to see
    the list of member names here.

Once you have selected values for numbers 1, 2, and 3, save the role
assignment.

You can use the role assignment capabilities to control the required
access to secrets, keys, or certificates.

In this lesson, we have discussed how we can handle access
management to Azure key vault.

Lesson 4.3: Using Key Vault to Save Keys

There are several security mechanisms you can use to protect data and
applications. The nature of the requirement decides the best security
mechanism to use. Disk encryption is technology that protects information
in the disk by converting information into unreadable code. If someone
has obtained the encryption keys, encrypted data can be read by them.
Therefore, it is mandatory to use secured vaults to keep the keys.

Azure key vault can be used to generate secure keys and keep the keys
securely.

Go to `https://portal.azure.com/` and log in as an administrator.

Select keys from the side setting blade and click on Generate/Import (see Figure 4-7).

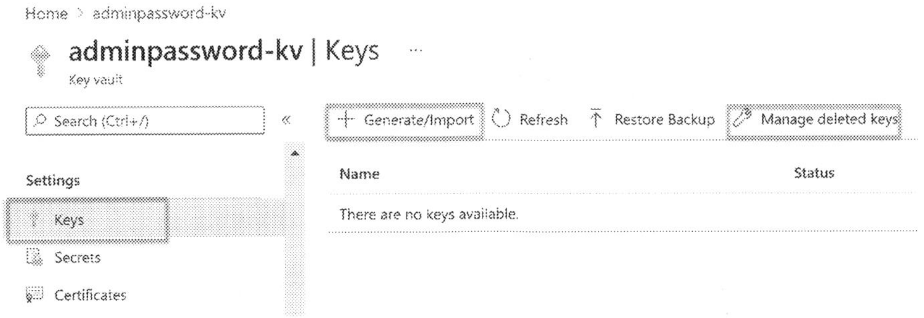

Figure 4-7. *Generate and import keys*

You can generate, import, or restore backup of keys. Let's learn one by one (see Figure 4-8).

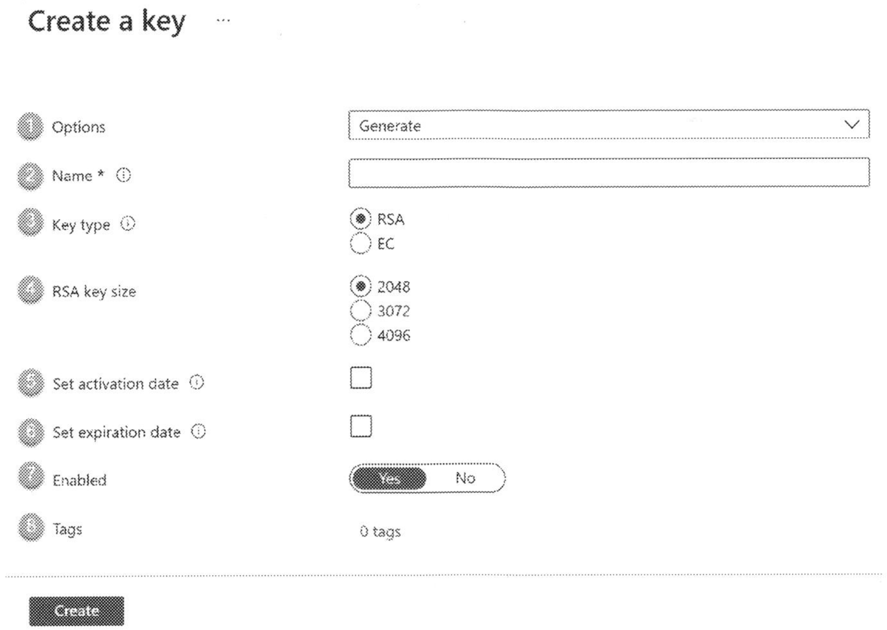

Figure 4-8. *Adding key*

1: Select the option from here.

Generate: You can generate new keys to use with information protection purposes.

Import: You can import the key value file and save it in the key vault using the import option.

Restore backup: You can use this option to restore a backup of key file

2: Provide name for the key.

3: Select the key type. You can select two types of keys.

RSA: RSA is a public-key encryption algorithm introduced by Ron Rivest, Adi Shamir, and Leonard Adleman in 1977 that uses acronyms from last names of the introducers. RSA is widely used for encryption in data secure transmissions.

EC: Elliptic-curve is cryptography based on the algebraic structure of elliptic curves over finite fields used to create public key cryptography.

4: RSA key size.

5, 6: You can select the activation date and expiration date for the key, which allows you to decide on a valid period to use the key.

7: You can set key as enabled or disabled.

Now you know how to create keys in the key vault. You can use the created key for several operations, such as encrypt, decrypt, sign, verify, wrap key, and unwrap key. Let's see how to use the key vault key to encrypt a virtual machine disk.

As a prerequisites, be sure that Azure virtual machine is up and running.

Go to the Azure VM overview page and click on disks from the side setting blade. From there, click on additional settings from the top right corner.

Select disks to encrypt.

Select key vault and key vault keys, which are required to do the disk encryption (see Figure 4-9).

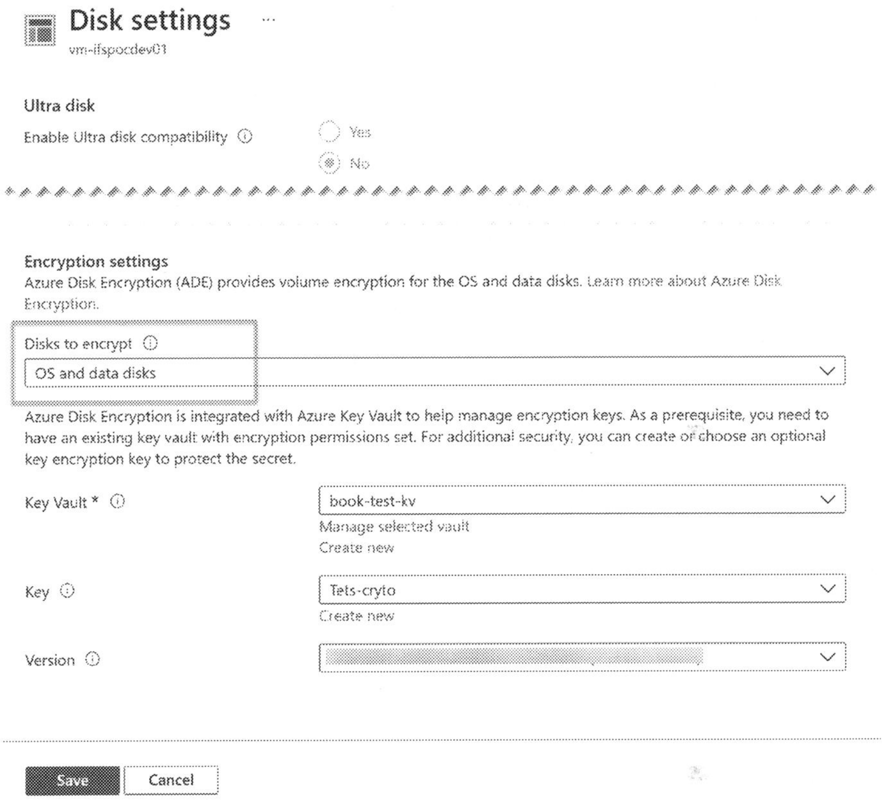

Disk settings ⋯
vm-ifspocdev01

Ultra disk

Enable Ultra disk compatibility ⓘ   ○ Yes
                             ◉ No

Encryption settings

Azure Disk Encryption (ADE) provides volume encryption for the OS and data disks. Learn more about Azure Disk Encryption.

Disks to encrypt ⓘ

| OS and data disks | ⌄ |

Azure Disk Encryption is integrated with Azure Key Vault to help manage encryption keys. As a prerequisite, you need to have an existing key vault with encryption permissions set. For additional security, you can create or choose an optional key encryption key to protect the secret.

Key Vault * ⓘ

| book-test-kv | ⌄ |

Manage selected vault
Create new

Key ⓘ

| Tets-cryto | ⌄ |

Create new

Version ⓘ

| ▓▓▓▓▓▓▓▓▓▓▓▓▓▓▓▓▓▓▓▓▓▓▓▓▓ | ⌄ |

| Save | Cancel |

Figure 4-9. *Disk encryption*

Disk encryption adds security to data stored inside the disk, and it is required to use keys to decrypt the encrypted data.

You have learned how to generate Azure key vault keys and use them from other Azure resources on encryption purposes in this lesson.

Lesson 4.4: Using Key Vault to Secure Secrets

Modern applications integrate with more third-party software and services, and such services require special secrets to gain accessibility by the service consumer application. Therefore, you need to use secrets in your applications to allow access to third-party services such as payment gateways, email, or other notification senders. Keeping your application secrets secure is an important aspect of application deployment specially on public clouds.

Let's learn how to work with Azure key vault secrets.

Go to `https://portal.azure.com/` and log in as an administrator.

Select secrets from the side setting blade. You will be able to see the secret creation page (see Figure 4-10).

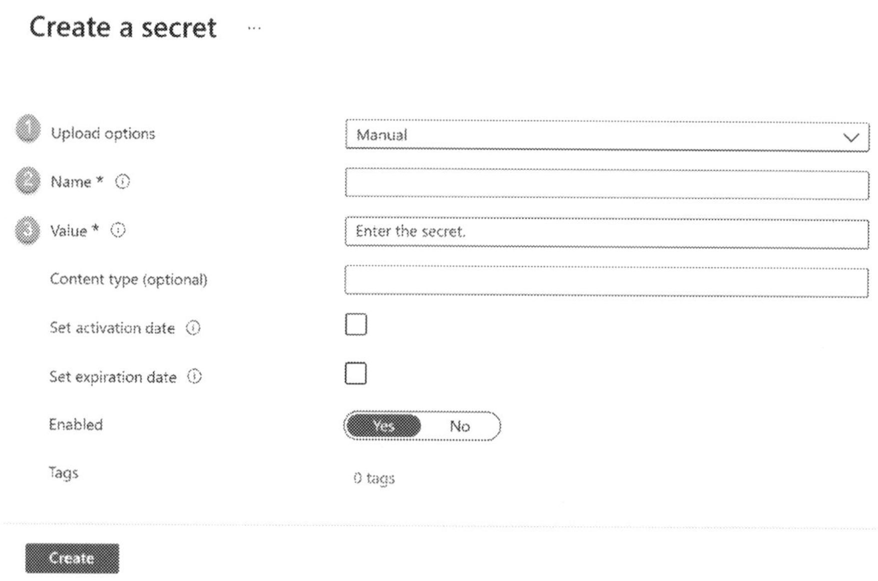

Create a secret ⋯

① Upload options		Manual ⌄
② Name * ⓘ		
③ Value * ⓘ		Enter the secret.
Content type (optional)		
Set activation date ⓘ	☐	
Set expiration date ⓘ	☐	
Enabled	Yes No	
Tags	0 tags	

Create

Figure 4-10. *Adding secret*

1. Select the Manual option to add value in portal while creating a secret.

2. Create a name for the secret.

3. Add the secret value, which is going to be saved in the key vault.

You can securely store the passwords under the secret section of Azure key vault. If the users have enough permission, they can directly read the secrets from the key vault or refer to the secret values from outside tools such as Azure DevOps pipeline, or App services.

You can consume Azure key vault stored secrets directly from Azure app services and function apps, under app settings. As the first step, you need to enable managed identity for your function app or app service (see Figure 4-11).

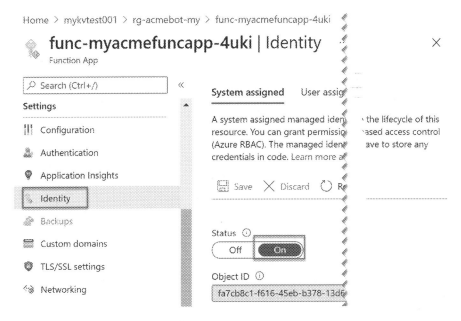

Figure 4-11. *Managing identity*

Then you can allow your app in key vault access policies to read and list secrets (see Figure 4-12).

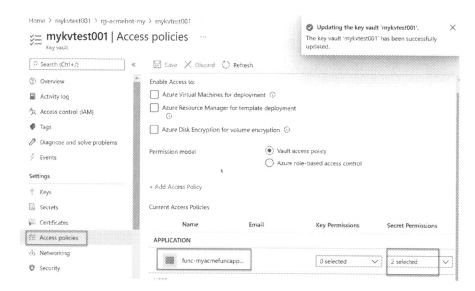

Figure 4-12. *Access policies*

Then you can refer to the key vault secret with the following syntax in your application app settings:

@Microsoft.KeyVault(VaultName=vaultname;SecretName=secretname; SecretVersion=secretVersion).

For example, secrets in Figure 4-13 can be accessed with:

@Microsoft.KeyVault(VaultName=mykvtest001;SecretName=mysecret
;SecretVersion=3f7b465451744652b3c66341f34bfd24)

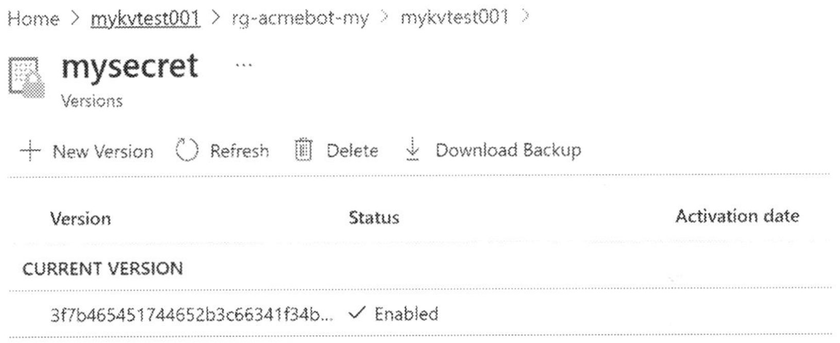

Home > <u>mykvtest001</u> > rg-acmebot-my > mykvtest001 >

mysecret ···
Versions

+ New Version   ◯ Refresh   🗑 Delete   ⬇ Download Backup

Version	Status	Activation date
CURRENT VERSION		
3f7b465451744652b3c66341f34b... ✓ Enabled		

Figure 4-13. *Secret value*

The application setting in the function app or app service will show
you the successful reference to key vault secret, as shown in Figure 4-14.

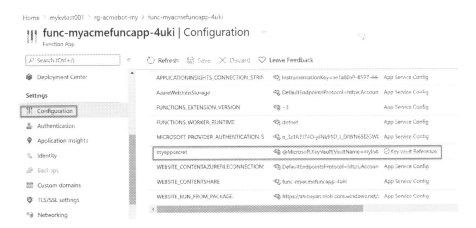

Figure 4-14. *Key vault reference from app setting*

You have learned how to add secret value to the Azure key vault in this lesson.

Lesson 4.5: Using Key Vault to Keep Certificates

Organizations can have multiple web services or multiple web projects that are developed for clients. Each of these sites should follow secured communication between web browsers and web servers. Secure Socket Layer (SSL) certificates are used to build up an encrypted communication between web browser and server. Otherwise, the important user details such as credit card information, usernames, and passwords can be stolen by hackers.

SSL certificates are important security components that need to be stored securely. Azure key vault has a section to store organization's certificates safely.

Let's learn how to utilize the Azure key vault certificates section.

Go to https://portal.azure.com/ and log in as an administrator.

Select secrets from the side setting blade. The certificate creation page will then be shown as Figure 4-15.

1. Certificates can be generated or can be imported to the key vault.

2. Provide the name of the certificate.

3. You can select the type of certificate authority from here.

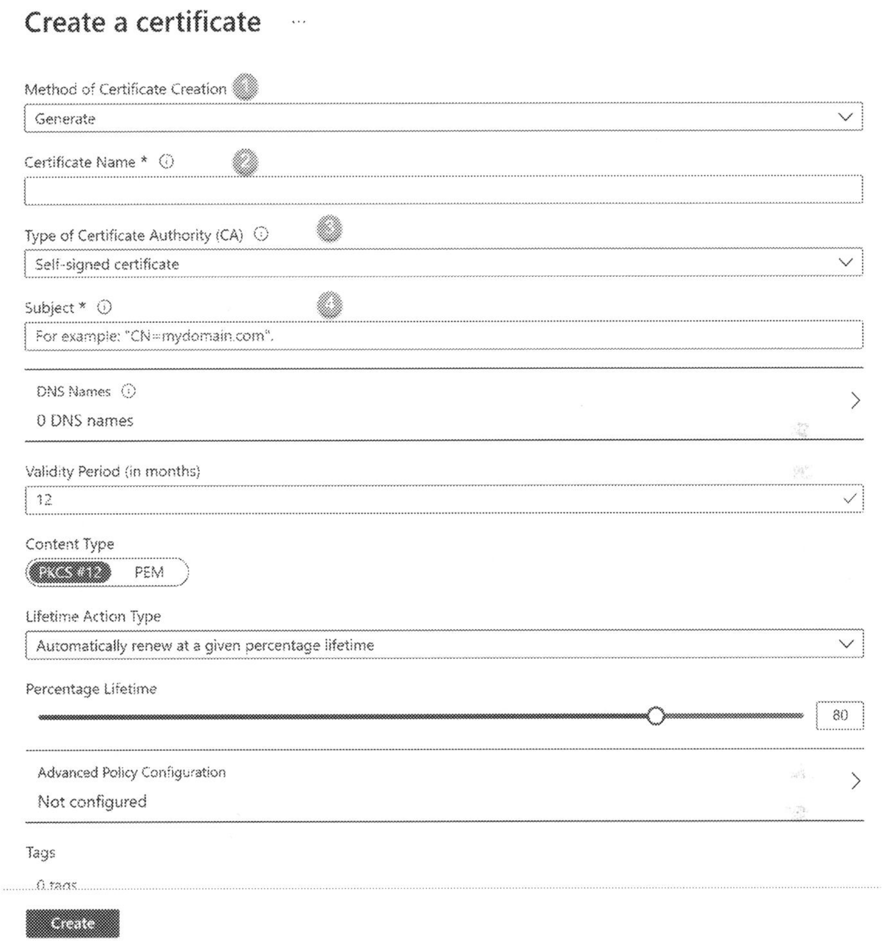

Create a certificate   ...

Method of Certificate Creation 🔵①
```
Generate                                                                    ∨
```

Certificate Name * ⓘ   🔵②
```

```

Type of Certificate Authority (CA) ⓘ   🔵③
```
Self-signed certificate                                                     ∨
```

Subject * ⓘ   🔵④
```
For example: "CN=mydomain.com".
```

DNS Names ⓘ   ＞
0 DNS names

Validity Period (in months)
```
12                                                                          ✓
```

Content Type
(PKCS #12   PEM)

Lifetime Action Type
```
Automatically renew at a given percentage lifetime                          ∨
```

Percentage Lifetime

───────────────────────○──────────── [80]

Advanced Policy Configuration   ＞
Not configured

Tags
0 tags

[Create]

Figure 4-15. *Creating a certificate*

Self-signed certificates: These certificates are not issued by any certificate authority. A smaller number of features are available when compared to Certification Authority issued (CA) certificates.

Certificates are issued by integrated CA and nonintegrated CA.

Nonintegrated CA is CA that is not partnered with Azure key vault. GoDaddy is a nonintegrated CA.

Integrated CA is CA partnered with key vault. DigiCert and GlobalSign are such integrated CAs.

4. CName, which is used to map domain names.

Other than the previously mentioned data, you can add the validity period for the certificate, which allows you to renew the certificate; this is good practice for maintaining the security of web services. You can also select the content type as Public Key Cryptography Standards (PKCS) or Privacy Enhanced Mail (PEM). It decides what information should be included in the certificate file.

In this lesson, we have discussed keeping certificates securely inside the Azure key vault.

Lesson 4.6: Key Vault Access Policies

Azure Key vault provides good security to the keys and other key vault objects that are stored in the vault. But key vault users can control the access policies to enhance the security of the values saved. There can be requirements which need to give key vault access to multiple users with multiple levels of permissions. Key vault values are secured by adding access policies which control who can do what with each key vault value. Let's learn how to work with access policies.

Go to https://portal.azure.com/ and log in as an administrator.

Select access policies from the side setting blade (see Figure 4-16).

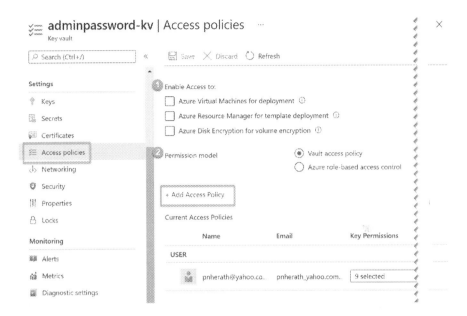

Figure 4-16. *Access policies*

Add access policies button to add policies to users, groups, or service principles to the resources. You can select what type of permission each user, group, or service connection gets for keys, secrets, and certificates. Mainly there are permissions such as Get, List, Update, Delete, Recover the keys, secrets, and certificates.

We have discussed the Azure key vault access policies in this lesson.

Lesson 4.7: Key Vault Networking and Security

Isolating the resources as much as possible is mandatory to secure the data and application of an organization. Controlling the access to the resource is one way of protecting the resource. Organizations can use networks to isolate the resources. Let's look at Azure key vault network and security.

Go to https://portal.azure.com/ and log in as an administrator.

Select networking from the side setting blade (see Figure 4-17).

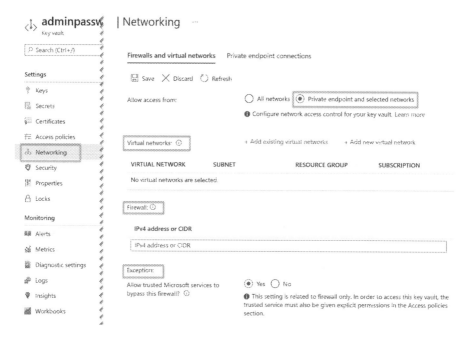

Figure 4-17. *Networking*

If all networks are selected, any permitted users can access the key vault from public networks. To prevent access from a public network, enable private endpoint and selected networks option. It will isolate the selected key vault and allow only permitted networks and end points to access it. Even if the user has permission inside the key vault, they cannot access the key vault without adding their device IP or access from inside the virtual network.

There is another option where you can allow trusted Microsoft services to bypass the firewall. These are the trusted services such as app services, function apps, and other services available in Azure cloud platform.

In this lesson we have discussed the network security aspect of Azure key vault.

Summary

This chapter explained the main features available with Azure Key vault and how it can be utilized to enhance the security of the data and applications of an organization. You will learn Azure features that provide application security in the next chapter.

CHAPTER 5

Ensuring Azure Application Security

Application security in respect to various aspects is vital in modern cloud-based solutions. Securing configuration information to ensure prevention of access to underlying services of an application by keeping such configuration hidden from outside access is required. Authentication and authorization mechanism with standard out-of-the-box identity providers is essential to keep your application functionality secured and accessed only by its intended users or services. Additionally, cloud utilization of network firewalls helps to control traffic and prevent malicious actions or hacking activities and attacks targeting your applications.

Lesson 5.1: Keeping Configurations in a Central Location Using Azure App Configuration

Organizations develop several web and desktop applications for their clients and for internal use. If an organization develops a product or project for their client, they need to have agreement on what type of information is shared among them. Sometimes organizations get access to client databases that contain a lot of confidential details that cannot

© Pushpa Herath 2022
P. Herath, *Azure Cloud Security for Absolute Beginners*,
https://doi.org/10.1007/978-1-4842-7860-4_5

be revealed publicly. Therefore, organizations have to use proper data and application security mechanisms even when they are developing the systems.

Having all the configuration data in one place is one of the development practices used by most developers. Normally config files have secret values, usernames, and passwords that should be stored securely. If you choose to save those config values in the development machines, this data might be easily accessed by unauthorized people. As a solution, Azure provides Azure configuration, which can be used as a central location for the app configurations. You can keep all the configuration values in the central location securely, which increases the security of your app development process and the application.

Let's learn how to create an Azure configuration.

Go to `https://portal.azure.com/` and log in as an administrator.

Search for Azure app configuration and select App Configuration from the search result (see Figure 5-1).

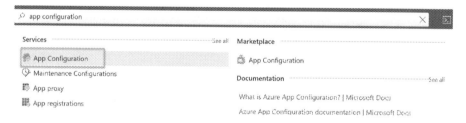

Figure 5-1. *App configuration*

You will be navigated to the App configuration page. Click on the create button to start the creation process (see Figure 5-2).

Create App Configuration   ...

Basics   Tags   Review + create

Azure App Configuration provides a service to centrally manage application settings an͏ ms, especially
programs running in a cloud, generally have many components that are distributed in ͏ · settings across
these components can lead to hard-to-troubleshoot errors during an application deplͤ ᵗo store all the
settings for your application and secure their accesses in one place. Learn more

Project Details

Subscription *   Microsoft Azure Sponsorship   ∨

⌐⋯⋯⋯⋯ Resource group *   ∨
                                       Create new

Instance Details

Resource name *   Enter resource name

Location *   East US   ∨

Pricing tier *   Standard   ∨
                                       View full pricing details

| Review + create | | < Previous | | Next: Tags > |

Figure 5-2. *Creating app configuration*

Select relevant subscriptions if you have multiple, select existing resource groups, or create a new one.

Enter a name for config app configuration service, select the location of the resource, and select the pricing for the resource. There are two pricing plans: free and standard.

The free plan is suitable for demonstration purposes, since it allows only very limited features. You can use the standard plan for enterprise purposes.

You can use tags and create the resource.

Now that we have explored how to create Azure app configuration, let's discuss the benefits of using Azure configurations for your applications.

The app configurations work as fully managed services that can be easily set up to be used with your applications. App configurations can be stored in a flexible representation of key value pairs. There is the possibility of retrieving app configuration values at a particular point of time, which can be useful in scenarios where it would be required to run some process in an application based on a previous configuration value, or to do an investigation on some configuration change.

It is possible to compare two sets of configurations in the purpose of diagnosing issues or audit purposes that enhance the security of the configurations. You can use Azure managed identities to secure access to Azure configurations from other Azure resources. Additionally, Azure configurations support encryption at REST and in transit, so that communication of stored configurations happens securely.

Azure key vault can be used in a seamless manner with Azure key vault to provide an extra level of security for your application keys and secrets. You can store secret Uniform Resource Identifier (URI) of key vault in App Configurations and obtain it securely using authenticating via managed identity. Then use the secret URI to obtain a secret value from the key vault, again using managed identity (see Figure 5-3).

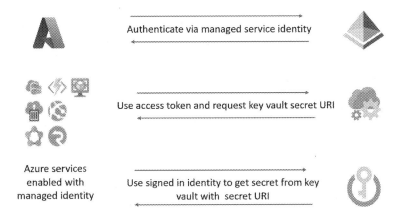

Figure 5-3. *Azure configurations and key vault*

We have discussed the use of Azure app configurations to securely store application configurations in this lesson.

Lesson 5.2: Authentication and Authorization in Azure App Service

App Services in Azure supports built-in authentication and authorization that enables you to implement utilizing minimal code in the web applications as well as REST APIs. The capabilities we discuss in this chapter are applicable to function apps and app service apps in Azure. Even though such built-in support exists, you can still use your own implementation for your web applications to secure them.

Why should we consider built-in authentication and authorization capabilities?

The built-in authentication can help you save time to focus on your application business requirements implementation, while handing over the authentication and authorization aspect to the federated identity providers. A variety of capabilities for authentication can be integrated without utilizing any particular language or Software development kit (SDKs), and you have the ability to use multiple login providers such as Azure AD, Google, Facebook and Twitter.

App Service with Azure AD Login

Let's explore how we can authenticate with Azure AD to access an Azure App Service deployed web application.

A a prerequisites, you should have Azure app service app set up in Azure. Copy your app service app URL (see Figure 5-4).

Figure 5-4. *Getting app URL*

Then open Azure active directory and select App registrations in the left menu. Click on new registration to create a new application registration (see Figure 5-5).

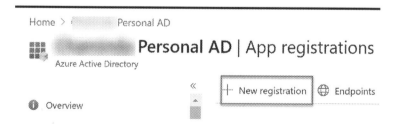

Figure 5-5. *New app registration*

In the register an application page, you should provide a name and the redirect URL should be set as your app service app URL. Register the new app registration (see Figure 5-6).

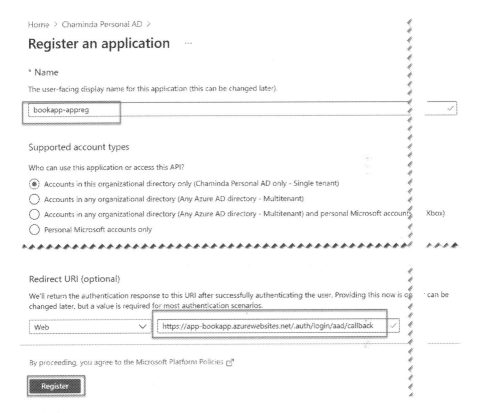

Figure 5-6. *Registering an application*

In the authentication section of the app registration, enable ID tokens to allow token-based authentication flows (see Figure 5-7).

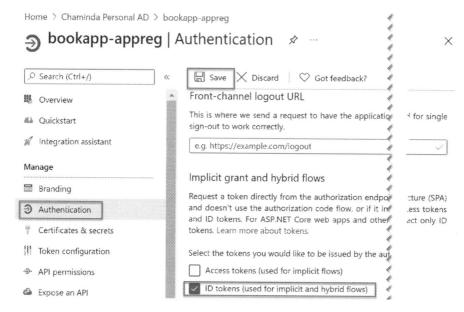

Figure 5-7. *Authentication*

In the Expose an API section, set an application ID URL (see Figure 5-8).

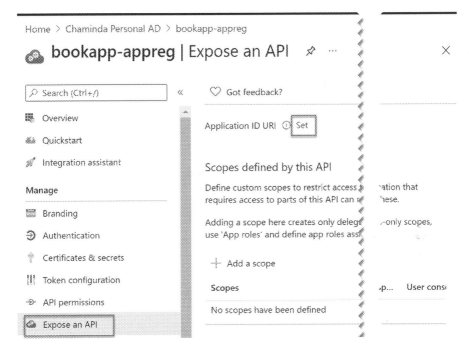

Figure 5-8. *Exposing an API*

Provide your Azure app service app URL and save (see Figure 5-9).

Figure 5-9. *Setting API URI*

Add scope and provide the scope name as user_impersonation. Provide consent messages and add the scope (see Figure 5-10).

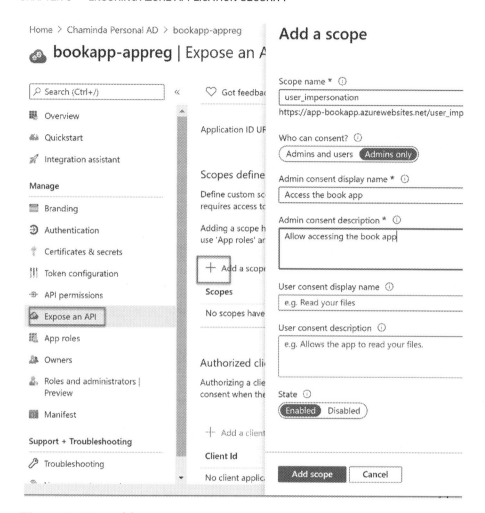

Figure 5-10. *Adding scope*

The next step is to enable authentication in your Azure app service app with the app registration created in the preceding steps. In the app authentication section, click on Add identity provider (see Figure 5-11).

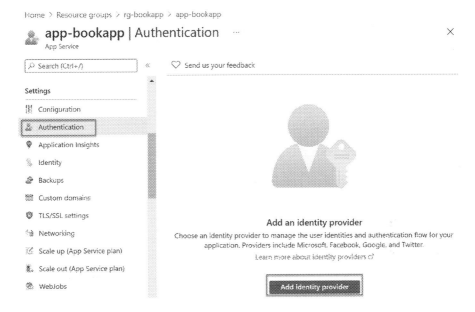

Figure 5-11. *Adding identity provider*

Select the identity provider as Microsoft, and then you can select the existing app registration that was created in earlier steps. The Issuer URL will be auto filled (see Figure 5-12).

Home > Resource groups > rg-bookapp > app-bookapp >

Add an identity provider   ...

Basics   Permissions

Identity provider *

| Microsoft   ∨ |

App registration

An app registration associates your identity provider with your app. Enter the app registration information here, or go to your provider to create a new one. Learn more ☝?

App registration type *   ○ Create new app registration

                                ◉ Pick an existing app registration in this directory

                                ○ Provide the details of an existing app registration

Name or app ID *

| bookapp-appreg (5c0366b4-1cb9-4ede-a0e9-cfe537f82843)   ∨ |

Issuer URL ⓘ

| https://sts.windows.net/efbad420-a8aa-4fcc-9e95-1d06435672d9/v2.0   ✓ |

> ⓘ A secret will be generated and added to the selected Azure Active Directory app registration. This value will be stored in
>   a configuration setting.

Figure 5-12. *AAD as identity provider*

Scroll down and select Require authentication. Set redirection on unattended requests and Add the identity provider to your app service app (see Figure 5-13).

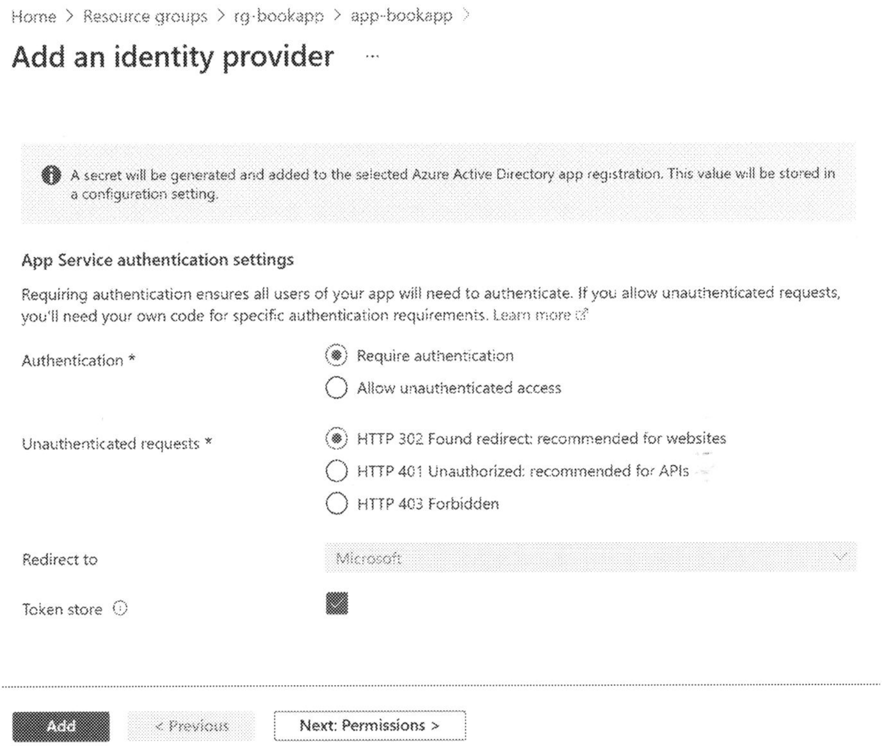

Home > Resource groups > rg-bookapp > app-bookapp >

Add an identity provider   ...

> ⓘ A secret will be generated and added to the selected Azure Active Directory app registration. This value will be stored in a configuration setting.

App Service authentication settings

Requiring authentication ensures all users of your app will need to authenticate. If you allow unauthenticated requests, you'll need your own code for specific authentication requirements. Learn more ◲

Authentication *	⦿ Require authentication
	◯ Allow unauthenticated access
Unauthenticated requests *	⦿ HTTP 302 Found redirect: recommended for websites
	◯ HTTP 401 Unauthorized: recommended for APIs
	◯ HTTP 403 Forbidden
Redirect to	Microsoft ⌄
Token store ⓘ	◼

[Add]   [< Previous]   [Next: Permissions >]

Figure 5-13. *Authentication settings*

Now you can launch your application in a browser and you will be prompted to log in. Once you log in with your Azure active directory account, you will be asked to accept permissions to access the app. Once accepted, you will be able to use the app (see Figure 5-14).

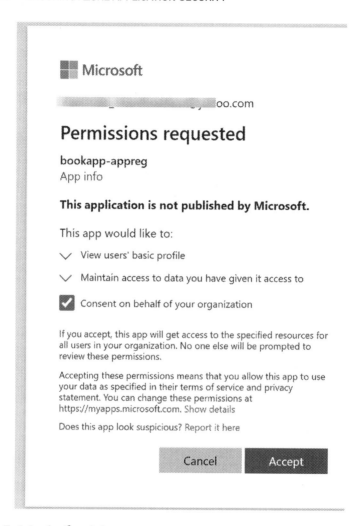

Figure 5-14. *Authorizing app*

The preceding steps explained how you can use a few simple steps to enable Azure AD-based authentication for your Azure app service apps without doing any sort of code implementation with out of the box identity providers.

Other Identity Providers

Similar to adding Azure AD as your app service app identity provider, you can configure Facebook, Google, or Twitter as well. Each of these providers allow you to set up authentication, and then you can use the provided client and secret information from the provider in your app service app to enable authentication. Azure app service apps support OpenId Connect Enabled Identity providers such as Identity Server 4.

Authentication Flows

Authentication flow depends on whether or not your application needs to use a provider SDK for authentication.

Not using provider SDK is typically implemented in browser apps that are capable of showing the provider's login page (for example Facebook or Microsoft) to the user. Once a user logs in, redirection happens to the Azure app service app.

In browser-less applications, the user will be signed in to the application via SDK programmatically and a token is submitted to the Azure app service for validation. The application code needs to manage the sign-in process using the provider's SDK. Typically, REST APIs would have to use SDK for implementing authentication with providers.

In addition to the points discussed previously, Azure app service has a built-in token store for your web apps APIs deployed to app service. Once you enable an authentication provider for your app service, the token store becomes available.

In this lesson we have explored Azure app service capability to work with authentication providers out of the box, with Azure AD as an example.

Lesson 5.3: Securing Application with Web Application Firewall in Azure

Cross-site scripting (XSS), cross-site forgery (CSRF), file inclusion, and SQL injection are common attacks targeting a web application. To avoid such attacks, a web application firewall is really useful. A web application firewall would essentially be filtering and monitoring the HTTP/HTTPS traffic between service and client.

Let's understand the difference between a firewall and a web application firewall. Firewalls operate in the layer 4 network, which is the transport layer and protects data transfer and network traffic based on ports, addresses, and protocols. However, such layer 4 firewalls do not protect the application. A web application firewall (WAF) works at layer 7 (application level) and protects web applications with HTTP/HTTPS traffic in addition to layer 4 protection. Therefore, a WAF is capable of protecting your web applications from attacks such as SQL injections, cookie manipulation, and cross-site scripting.

In Azure you have an application gateway and an Azure front door as web application firewalls. Both implementations share some common overlapping functionalities and can be used to protect HTTP/HTTPS traffic and act as a load balancer for back-end servers. Azure front door is a global service and Azure application gateway is a regional service, which is the main difference between the two offerings. Azure front door allows you to manage global routing to your application across regions, whereas Azure application gateway allows you to manage routing for a single region. This means that if your web application is set up in a region in Australia and if a user from the United States tries to access it, the traffic would go over public Internet until it reaches Australia datacenter if the implementation is done with Azure application gateway. As Azure front door is a global service with software-based networking, deployed at Microsoft's edge locations around the world. When a user in the United States tries to access the website in the Australia region, once the traffic reaches the edge location in the United States the rest of the traffic routes through Microsoft backbone network, making the user experience much faster. You can use the Azure front door and application gateway together where the front door does load balancing at global level.

Web application firewalls can be configured to operate in two modes: detection mode and in prevention mode. In detection mode WAF will monitor and log all the threats and will not block incoming requests. However, when you set it to prevention mode, WAF starts to block any attacks or intrusions, actively sending 403 unauthorized access to the attacker. Prevention mode also logs the attack information.

Azure application gateway has two SKUs, Waf and WAF V2. The additional benefits of using WAF V2 over WAF are in allowing autoscaling eliminating the need to set the capacity at peak, more resilient with zone redundancy surviving zonal failures, faster provisioning, static virtual IPs, improved performance, and the ability to update, add, or remove HTTP request headers facilitating securing cookies and other items without changing application code.

As you can see in Figure 5-15, once you set up WAF policies and rules any attack that is coming toward your application will be prevented by the firewall. Valid requests will be forwarded to the application to serve.

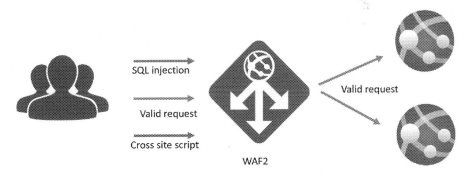

Figure 5-15. *WAF2*

Let's explore a couple of important aspects of the Azure application gateway to get an understanding of how it should be configured. We should have an understanding of back-end pools, listeners, http settings, rules, health probes, and back-end health to have a basic configuration done in application gateway (see Figure 5-16).

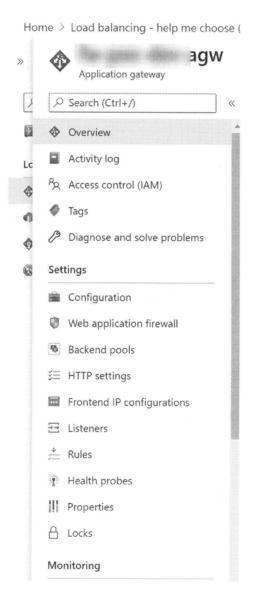

Figure 5-16. *Application gateway*

In the web application firewall section of the application gateway, you can define configuration for the WAF. As we discussed previously, you can set up mode for detection or prevention and add additional settings such as parameters to inspect a request body, or items to exclude from inspection (see Figure 5-17).

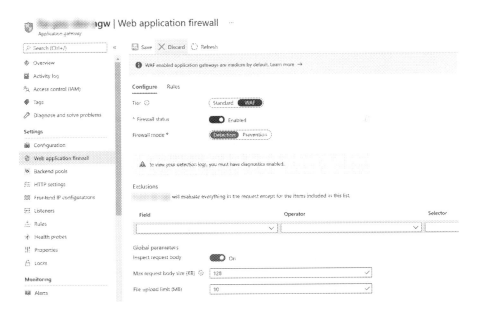

Figure 5-17. *WAF*

The rules section can be used to set up the rules for web application firewalls, and advanced setup allows you to further configure rules for your preferences and needs (see Figure 5-18).

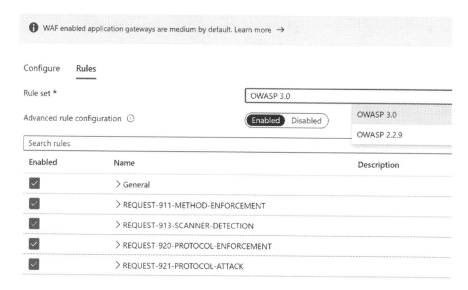

Figure 5-18. *Rules*

Front end IP configurations allow you to set up public or private IP
configurations for your application gateway. Public IP allows access to
the application gateway via a public IP where you can use private IP and
configure your app gateway inside a virtual network in Azure, allowing
access only via virtual network or from any other peer virtual networks (see
Figure 5-19).

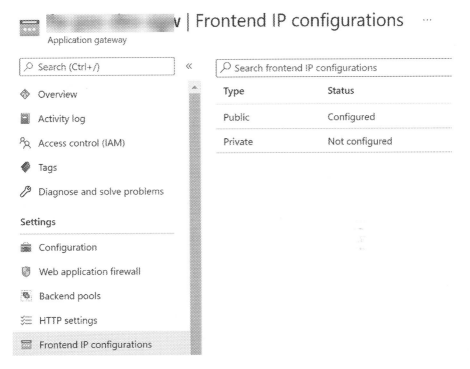

Figure 5-19. *Front-end IPs*

Back-end pool is where you configure your web application, function app, or a virtual machine as a back-end resource protected and load-balanced by the application gateway. In the back-end pool you can specify your Azure web app as back-end target by selecting target type as app service. Additionally, virtual machines, virtual machine scale sets, or a fully qualified domain name (FQDN) can be set up as targets (see Figure 5-20).

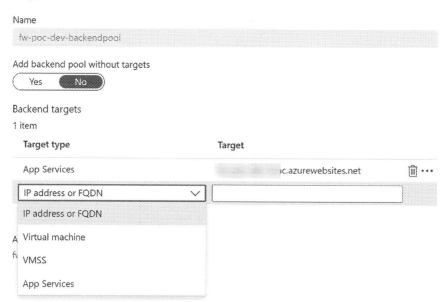

Figure 5-20. *Back-end pool*

Health probes can be defined so you can use them in back-end pool targets health status checks. Based on the probe, setting back-end targets will be verified for connectivity state (see Figure 5-21).

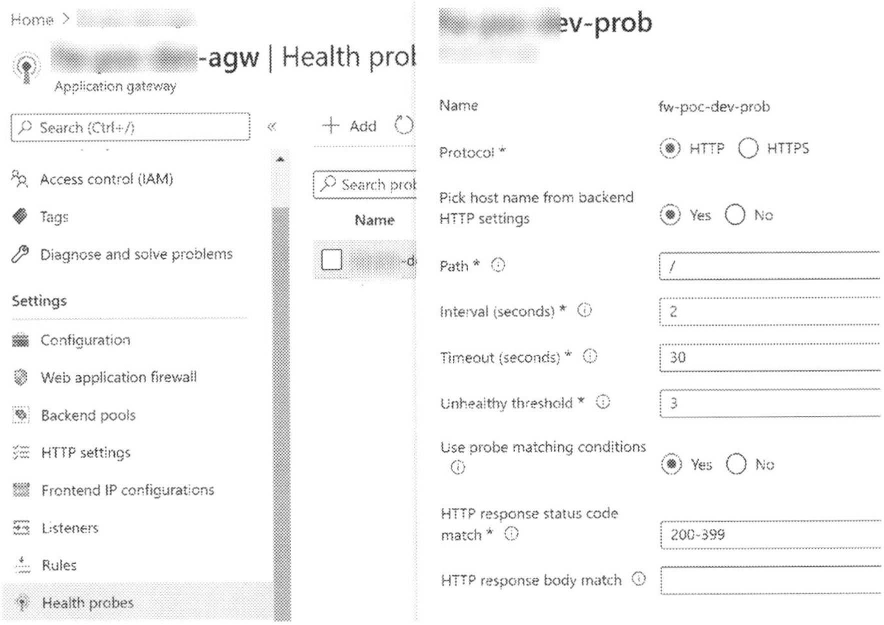

Figure 5-21. *Health probe*

Listeners can be configured to listen for the incoming request in the application gateway. You can use public IP or private IP, specify port, and protocol as HTTP or HTTPS. A listener will be associated with a rule, which we will look at later in this lesson. A listener can be a multisite listener that can route to multiple back-end targets, or it can be a basic listener only routing to a single target based on the rule (see Figure 5-22).

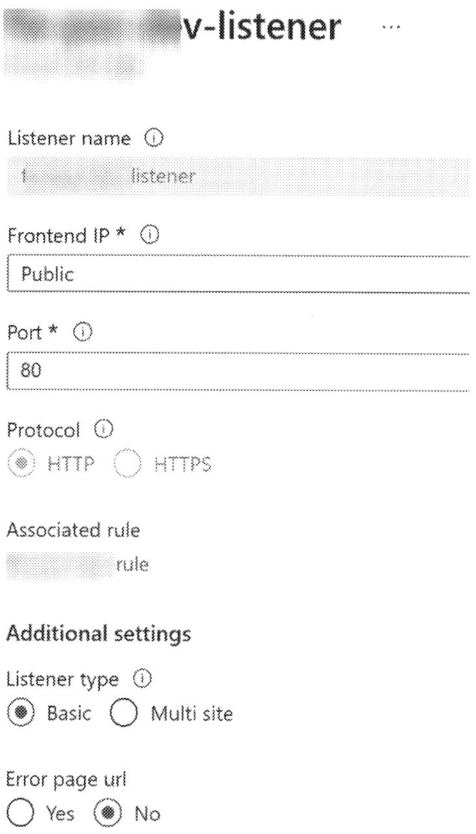

v-listener ⋯

Listener name ⓘ

listener

Frontend IP * ⓘ

Public

Port * ⓘ

80

Protocol ⓘ
◉ HTTP ◯ HTTPS

Associated rule

rule

Additional settings

Listener type ⓘ
◉ Basic ◯ Multi site

Error page url
◯ Yes ◉ No

Figure 5-22. Listener

A rule can be specified with a listener and using back-end targets (see Figure 5-23).

-dev-rule

Configure a routing rule to send traffic from a given frontend IP address to one or more backend targets. A routing rule must contain a listener and at least one backend target.

Rule name

* **Listener**   * Backend targets

A listener "listens" on a specified port and IP address for traffic that uses a specified protocol. If the listener criteria are met, the application gateway will apply this routing rule.

Listener *

Figure 5-23. *Rule listener*

Back-end target of a rule can be defined as a back-end pool by specifying the back-end target and HTTP settings (see Figure 5-24).

c-dev-rule

-agw

Configure a routing rule to send traffic from a given frontend IP address to one or more backend targets. A routing rule must contain a listener and at least one backend target.

Rule name

* Listener   * **Backend targets**

Choose a backend pool to which this routing rule will send traffic. You will also need to specify a set of HTTP settings that define the behavior of the routing rule.

Target type   ● Backend pool ○ Redirection

Backend target * ⓘ   -backendpool

HTTP settings * ⓘ   -httpsetting

Figure 5-24. *Rule back-end pool*

Or, you can define the rule so as to work as a redirection to a target. Such a redirection target can be another listener or an external site (see Figure 5-25).

117

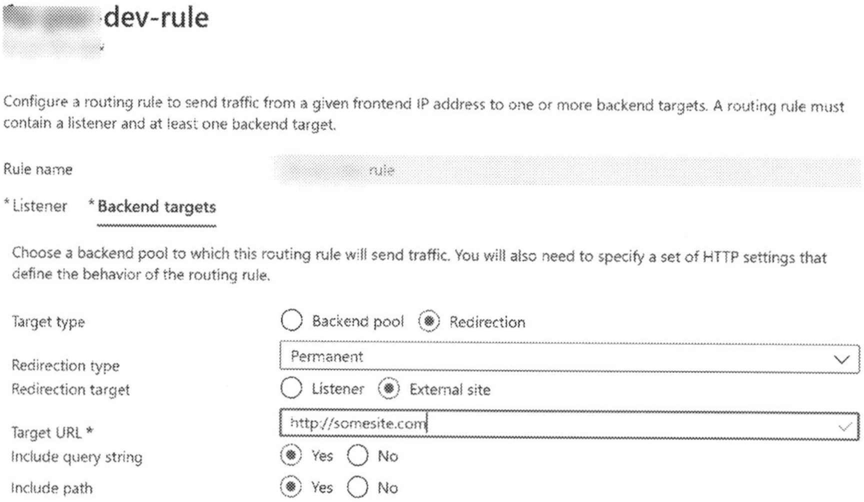

░░░░dev-rule

Configure a routing rule to send traffic from a given frontend IP address to one or more backend targets. A routing rule must contain a listener and at least one backend target.

Rule name   rule

* Listener   * **Backend targets**

Choose a backend pool to which this routing rule will send traffic. You will also need to specify a set of HTTP settings that define the behavior of the routing rule.

Target type   ◯ Backend pool ⦿ Redirection

Redirection type   Permanent   ⌄
Redirection target   ◯ Listener ⦿ External site

Target URL *   http://somesite.com   ⌄
Include query string   ⦿ Yes ◯ No

Include path   ⦿ Yes ◯ No

Figure 5-25. *Redirection*

We have explored some configuration settings of application gateway to give you a good understanding of setting up to secure your applications.

In this lesson we have discussed the use of WAF and the available Azure WAF implementations that can be used to protect your web applications.

Lesson 5.4: Application Security Group

Application security groups is the application centric implementation of network security groups where you are allowed to manage security of virtual machines grouped together based on the applications running on them. The logical grouping of virtual machines can be done to application security groups regardless of the subnet or IP address assignment of the virtual machines within a given virtual network.

Network security group (NSG) is generally assigned to a subnet or a network identification (NIC). Once you have the NSG rules defined, they would apply to all the NICs in the subnet. When you are deploying a new system you can easily group your virtual machines into subnets and use NSGs to apply the network rules, considering them as individual security zones. However, in real-world scenarios where your virtual machines are not ideally grouped logically to subnets according to the security needs of the applications running on them, you might find it difficult to apply the NSG rules for a subnet. There should be a more flexible way for you to logically group your virtual machines, regardless of the subnet they are deployed on and apply the security rules. Application security groups (ASG) come in handy in this situation, allowing you to group your virtual machines logically across subnets.

ASGs allow us to define security policies based on the workloads of the applications deployed into virtual machines via NSG. You can filter traffic to your applications using ASGs, allowing you to protect your application workloads in isolation. The flexibility of application security groups lets us define the scope of security based on applications or environments such as development, QA or production, or any other kind of custom role specification.

You can define a single NSG for your virtual network and create application security groups as needed to apply across multiple subnets, making the security policy implementation more flexible and manageable. A virtual machine can be assigned with multiple ASGs, allowing you to have different workloads deployed in a given virtual machine and apply security accordingly.

Application security groups can be termed as a logical collection of your virtual machines network identifications (NICs). You can set up ASGs and use them in your NSG as source and destination, making your rules apply to source and destination ASGs. By configuring with NSG, the rules you define in NSG can be applied to any virtual machine linked with the ASG (see Figure 5-26).

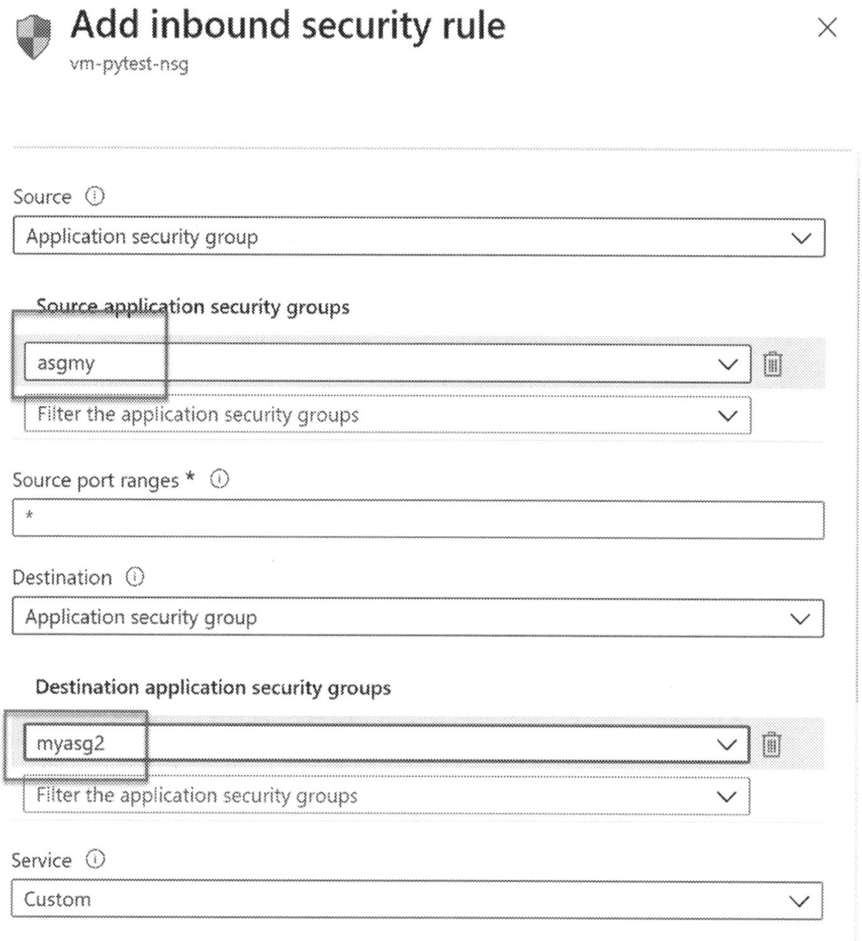

Add inbound security rule   ✕

vm-pytest-nsg

Source ⓘ

| Application security group | ⌄ |

Source application security groups

| asgmy | ⌄ | 🗑 |

| Filter the application security groups | ⌄ |

Source port ranges * ⓘ

| * |

Destination ⓘ

| Application security group | ⌄ |

Destination application security groups

| myasg2 | ⌄ | 🗑 |

| Filter the application security groups | ⌄ |

Service ⓘ

| Custom | ⌄ |

Figure 5-26. *Using ASGs for NSG rules*

Then each of your virtual machine network identification in the network blade can be assigned with the application security group. For associating multiple ASGs you need multiple NICs in your VM (see Figure 5-27).

Figure 5-27. *Assigning ASG to NIC of a VM*

As we have explored in this section, ASGs can be defined and assigned to virtual machines across subnets, and utilized in NSG rules as source and destination applying a set of rules defined in NGS to a particular ASG, applying to one or more virtual machines via virtual machine NIC. Such configuration allows for easy management of network rules and applies security in a manageable way based on application workloads.

In this lesson we have explored the application security groups and its use.

Summary

In this chapter we have discussed the use of Azure application configurations to securely store application configuration. Additionally, we have explored the authentication and authorization providers supported out of the box for Azure app services, and looked at how a simple implementation works to secure an application deployed to Azure app service with zero code changes using Azure AD as an identity provider. The use of web application firewalls were discussed to understand how to further enhance the application security, and we have explored application security groups that facilitate security rules based on application workloads deployed to virtual machines.

In the next chapter, let's discuss Azure storage security.

CHAPTER 6

Ensuring Data Security with Azure Storage

Organizations work with a large amount of data daily which are required to provide services to their clients and internal functionalities. Storing data such as images and documents in databases was often found in legacy applications. However, modern architecture patterns do not recommend storing such binary data, especially larger files, in databases because they hinder the performance of the database and increase cost due its size. Therefore, modern solutions recommend that documents, images, and video files uploaded as application data be stored in storage accounts and outside of databases.

Managing and securing large amounts of data is a challenge for any type of organization due to cyber-attack vulnerabilities and security vulnerabilities of an organization. As the solution for these security threats and management, Azure has introduced Azure storages. Azure storage provides a scalable object store for various data objects and services. Azure storage is secure, scalable, accessible, and durable storage for data storage requirements of organizations.

© Pushpa Herath 2022
P. Herath, *Azure Cloud Security for Absolute Beginners*,
https://doi.org/10.1007/978-1-4842-7860-4_6

Lesson 6.1: Setting Up Azure Storage

Let's learn how to set up an Azure storage account.

Go to https://portal.azure.com/ and log in as an administrator.

Search for storage account and click on storage account in the search result, and to go to storage account creation page (see Figure 6-1).

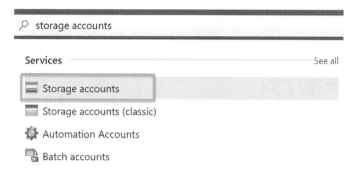

Figure 6-1. *Searching storage*

Click on the create button to start the storage account creation process. You will be able to see the first step of the storage creation process (see Figure 6-2).

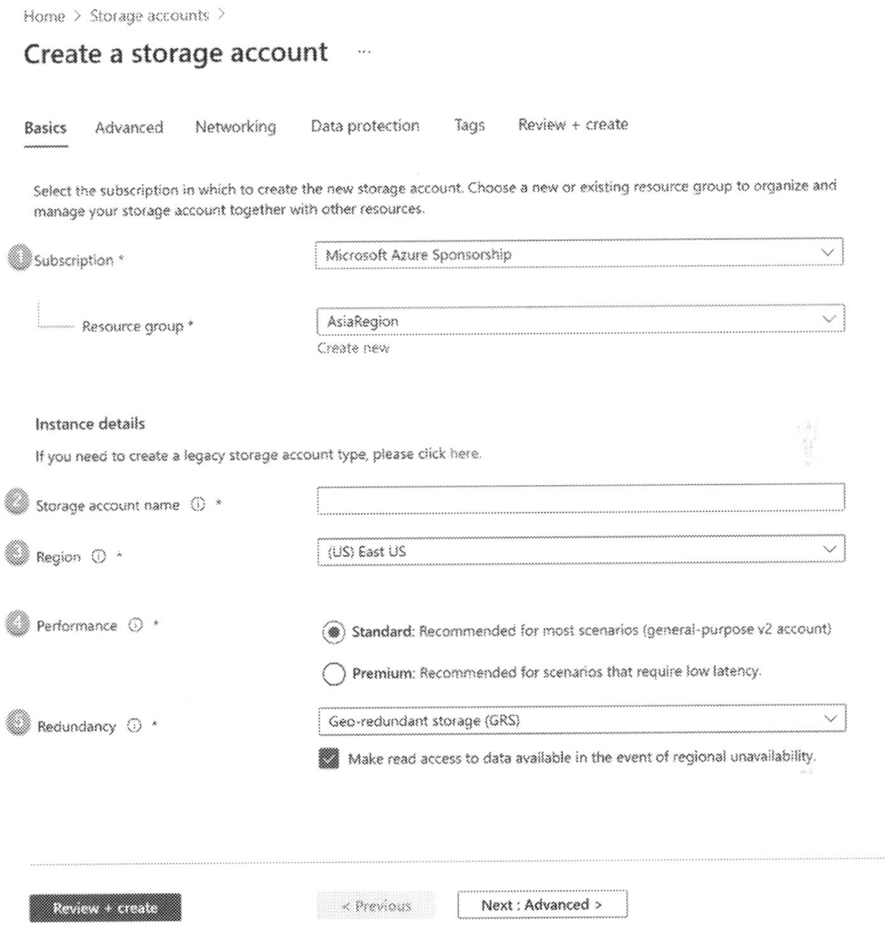

Home > Storage accounts >

Create a storage account   ...

Basics   Advanced   Networking   Data protection   Tags   Review + create

Select the subscription in which to create the new storage account. Choose a new or existing resource group to organize and manage your storage account together with other resources.

Subscription *

| Microsoft Azure Sponsorship | ∨ |

Resource group *

| AsiaRegion | ∨ |

Create new

Instance details

If you need to create a legacy storage account type, please click here.

Storage account name ⓘ *

| |

Region ⓘ *

| (US) East US | ∨ |

Performance ⓘ *

◉ **Standard:** Recommended for most scenarios (general-purpose v2 account)

○ **Premium:** Recommended for scenarios that require low latency

Redundancy ⓘ *

| Geo-redundant storage (GRS) | ∨ |

☑ Make read access to data available in the event of regional unavailability.

[Review + create]   < Previous   [Next : Advanced >]

Figure 6-2. *Storage account*

1. Select the relevant subscription if there are multiple subscriptions. Select the resource group where you need to create the storage account or create a new resource group.

2. Add the storage account name.

3. Select the region for the storage account.

4. You can select the type of the storage account as premium or standard, according to requirements. If there are low latency critical workloads, premium is recommended.

5. Redundancy is an important feature in Azure storage that ensures the availability of the data. It stores multiple copies of data to make sure of its availability when there are network and power failures, natural disasters, or any other unintended or intended events.

Once all mandatory fields have been selected and filled, move to the Advanced section (see Figure 6-3).

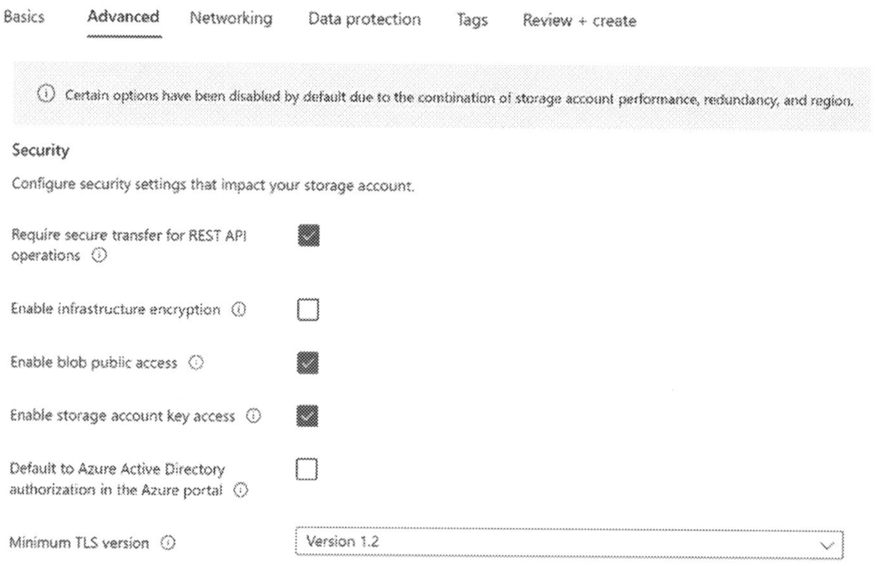

Figure 6-3. *Storage account advanced*

You can configure security settings in the Advanced tab.

Require secure transfer for REST API operations: This allows REST API operations on storage using only HTTPS. Once this feature is enabled, any requests coming from an insecure connection are rejected. Further, unencrypted Azure file service connections will fail.

Enable infrastructure encryption: By default, storage has service level encryption for securing the data inside. However, if users need an extra security layer they can enable this feature, which adds an extra security layer by adding encryption to the infrastructure level.

Enable blob public access: This feature allows anonymous access to storage blobs. However, users can enhance the security by avoiding the public access to blob by disabling this feature.

Enable storage account key access: If this feature is disabled, any request authorized with a shared key will be denied.

Default to Azure Active Directory authorization in the Azure portal: This feature enables the Azure active directory authorization for request to blobs, queues, and tables.

Minimum TLS version: TLS is required for secure communication between web browsers and servers. However, if outdated TLS is used, it adds vulnerabilities to security and data transmitted using TLS. Therefore, selecting the correct TLS version is important for the security of data. This feature allows users to select the minimum TLS version needed for communication between storage data and applications.

Advanced settings can also be set as shown in Figure 6-4.

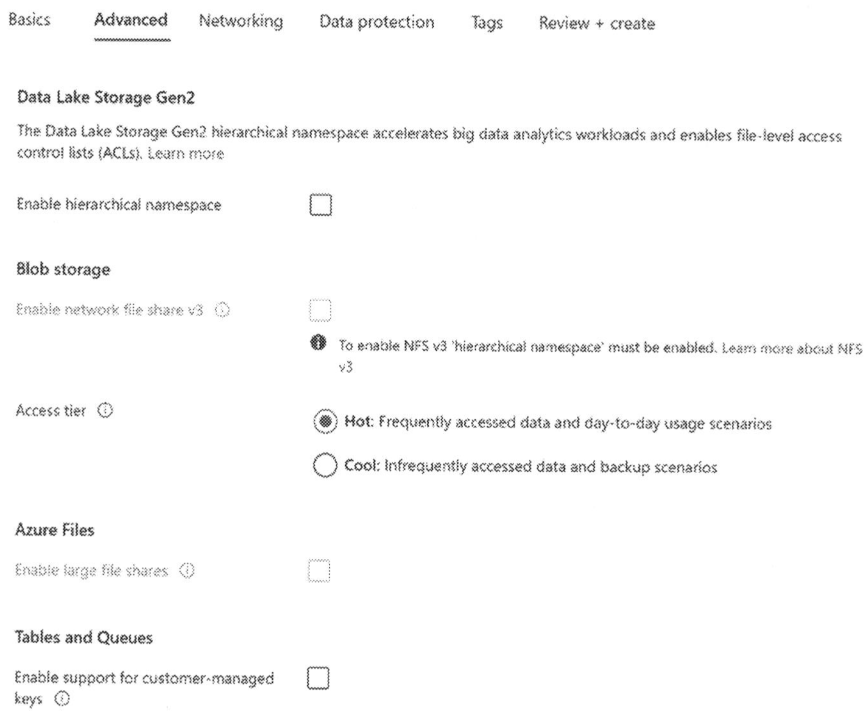

Basics   **Advanced**   Networking   Data protection   Tags   Review + create

Data Lake Storage Gen2

The Data Lake Storage Gen2 hierarchical namespace accelerates big data analytics workloads and enables file-level access
control lists (ACLs). Learn more

Enable hierarchical namespace   ☐

Blob storage

Enable network file share v3 ⓘ   ☐

❶ To enable NFS v3 'hierarchical namespace' must be enabled. Learn more about NFS
v3

Access tier ⓘ   ⦿ **Hot:** Frequently accessed data and day-to-day usage scenarios

                                             ◯ **Cool:** Infrequently accessed data and backup scenarios

Azure Files

Enable large file shares ⓘ   ☐

Tables and Queues

Enable support for customer-managed   ☐
keys ⓘ

Figure 6-4. *Advanced security*

Data Lake Storage Gen2: To use the storage with Azure Data Lake
Storage Gen2, you need to enable the hierarchical namespace. This
configuration allows Azure storage to service for multiple petabytes
of **data.**

Enable network file share v3: Enabling this setting provides Linux file
system compatibility, allowing mounting in the storage in a Linux VM or
on-premise computers.

Access tier: Access tire in storage account allows you to store data
in the most cost-effective manner for your application data needs. For

frequently accessed data you can use hot tier, and you can use cool tier for infrequently accessed data.

Enable large file shares: You can enable this feature for standard LRS (local redundant storage) or ZRS (zone redundant storage) to use larger file shares.

Enable support for customer-managed keys: To use custom managed keys with storage tables and queues, you must enable this setting at the time of creation of the storage account.

You have learned the advanced settings available with storage. Let's move to the networking tab for network configurations (see Figure 6-5).

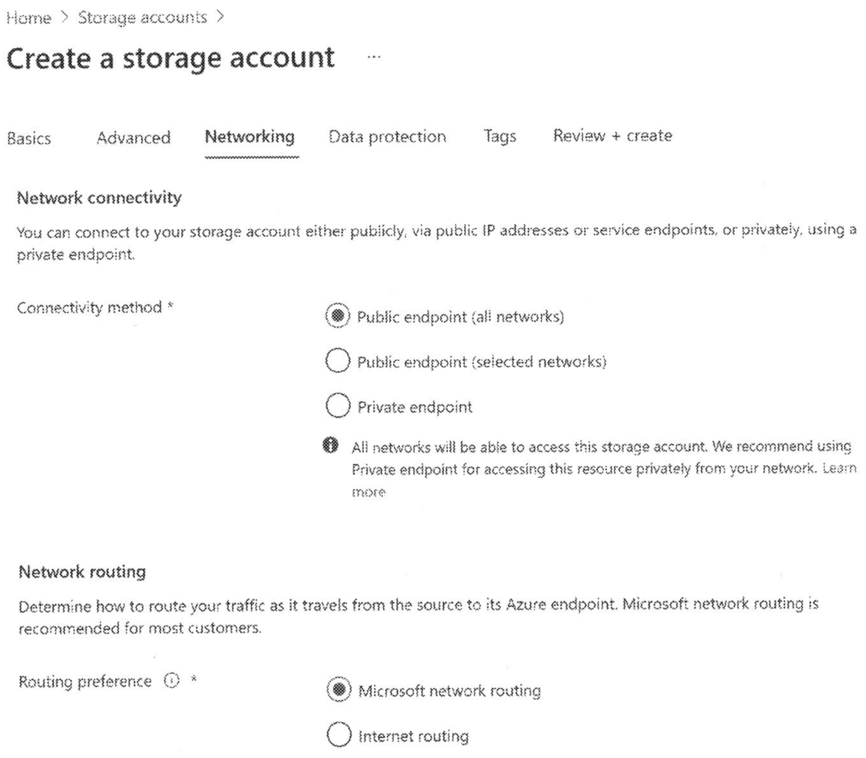

Home > Storage accounts >

Create a storage account   ...

Basics   Advanced   Networking   Data protection   Tags   Review + create

Network connectivity

You can connect to your storage account either publicly, via public IP addresses or service endpoints, or privately, using a private endpoint.

Connectivity method *

◉ Public endpoint (all networks)

◯ Public endpoint (selected networks)

◯ Private endpoint

⦿ All networks will be able to access this storage account. We recommend using Private endpoint for accessing this resource privately from your network. Learn more

Network routing

Determine how to route your traffic as it travels from the source to its Azure endpoint. Microsoft network routing is recommended for most customers.

Routing preference ⓘ *

◉ Microsoft network routing

◯ Internet routing

Figure 6-5. *Storage networking*

Incoming traffic to the storage account routes via public endpoint by default, allowing incoming traffic from any network. You can restrict this to happen via Azure virtual network by setting it as a public endpoint with selected network. To further strengthen the security, you can enable private endpoints and configure a private endpoint in Azure.

You can select the preferred routing as Microsoft network routing, which routes the calls to storage public endpoint by default. Internet routing will direct to the closest POP (point of presence), which may effectively lower the networking costs.

You can store your data in Azure storage securely. However, there can be unintended data deletion from Storages. When such a situation occurs, Azure Storage has recovery features available for protecting the data (see Figure 6-6).

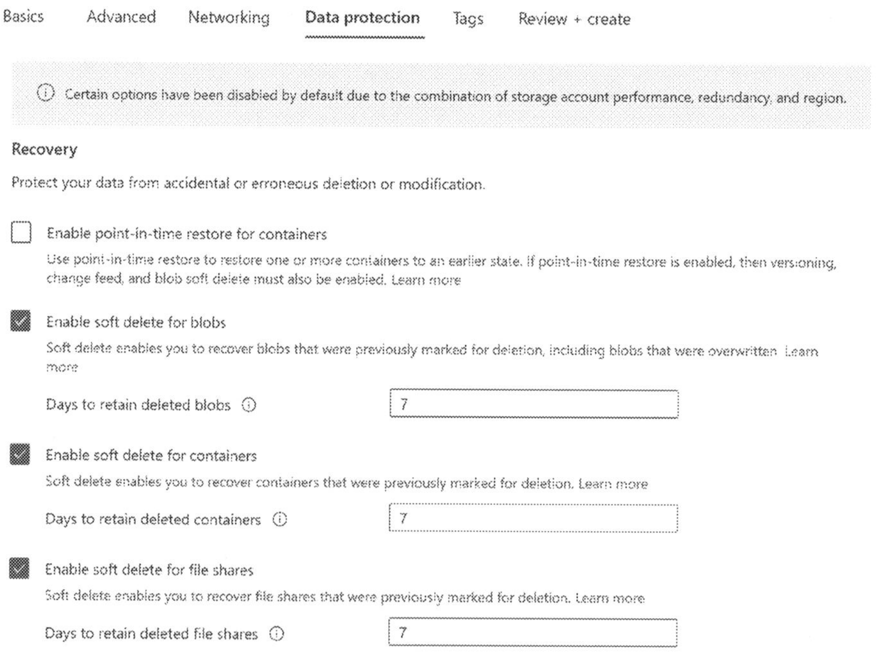

Figure 6-6. *Data protection*

Enable point-in-time restore for containers: This feature allows you to restore your blob containers to a particular point in time, facilitating recovery from corrupted data states by restoring to a previous version.

Enable soft delete for blobs: Soft deletion allows deleted blob data to be recovered/restored within the specified soft deletion period.

Enable soft delete for containers: Soft deletion allows deleted container data to be recovered/restored within the specified soft deletion period.

Enable soft delete for file shares: Soft deletion allows deleted file share data to be recovered/restored within the specified soft deletion period.

Such soft deletions allow recovery of data deleted from malfunctions of your application logic, accidental deletions by users, or intentional malicious activities, providing additional capability to have a resilient data store.

Organizations have to manage huge amounts of data and need continuous modifications and updates. However, it is an important but difficult task to keep track of the changes done to files. Azure storage has a track feature to track changes made to blobs, which helps users to track the blob changes (see Figure 6-7).

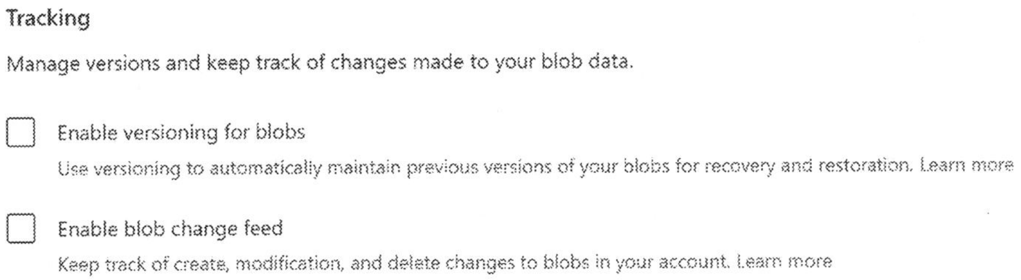

Tracking

Manage versions and keep track of changes made to your blob data.

☐ Enable versioning for blobs
Use versioning to automatically maintain previous versions of your blobs for recovery and restoration. Learn more

☐ Enable blob change feed
Keep track of create, modification, and delete changes to blobs in your account. Learn more

Figure 6-7. *Storage tracking*

Enable versioning for blobs: Blob content is versioned, and it is possible to view history and revert back to a previous version of data.

Enable blob change feed: This will track the information about the changes to blobs and metadata in blob transaction logs.

Once all required fields are filled and selected, you can create a new storage account.

We have discussed how to create an Azure storage and what security components can be utilized to secure the data inside the storage. Let's consider how to use Azure storage in application development to enhance the data security of an application.

Shopping cart or video streaming sites such as Netflix have several files that store several details. Those can be image files, pdf or text files, video files, and more. When there are more and more files in the system developers need to store these data securely, but the storage mechanism should not affect the performance of the system. As a solution, Azure storage can be used to store image files, video files, and other required files securely that cannot be accessed by unauthorized users. Application will be the only way of accessing images and other files. Storage accounts have capability limit access to a virtual network where your application resides. You can add all the application file and media data into the storage and open a dedicated secure channel for the application to access the storage data. Therefore, anyone outside the network cannot access the storage data, making the only way to access storage data via the application. Another use of storage account is that you can mount storage to a virtual machine disk to increase the storage capacity of the virtual machine.

In this lesson, we have looked at a couple of storage account creation options and what we can enable as features to enable enhanced security.

Lesson 6.2: Azure Storage Encryption

Azure storage by default is enabled with encryption for all storage accounts, which is transparent to the users. It works similar to BitLocker encryption in Windows. You are not allowed to disable the encryption in Azure storages, which ensures safety of your data. Encryption works the same way regardless of the performance tier or access tier of the storage accounts.

Additionally, infrastructure level encryption can be enabled in storage, providing double encryption for data stored. You can set up Azure policy to demand for infrastructure encryption so that all of the storage accounts created in a subscription(s) are enforced to apply an additional layer of encryption for enhanced security. However, infrastructure encryption can only be enabled at the creation time of the storage account, as described in the previous lesson.

Let's go to Azure storage to learn a bit about the encryption settings. You will be able to find encryption settings in the side settings blade of the storage account (see Figure 6-8).

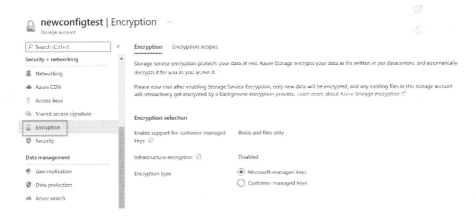

Figure 6-8. *Encryption settings*

You can find the details of the encryption mechanism used in the storage. If there is a requirement to use a customer managed key, it can be selected from the encryption page. You can also define encryption scope, such as whether to enable infrastructure level encryption or not, in the encryption scope creation page (as shown in Figure 6-9).

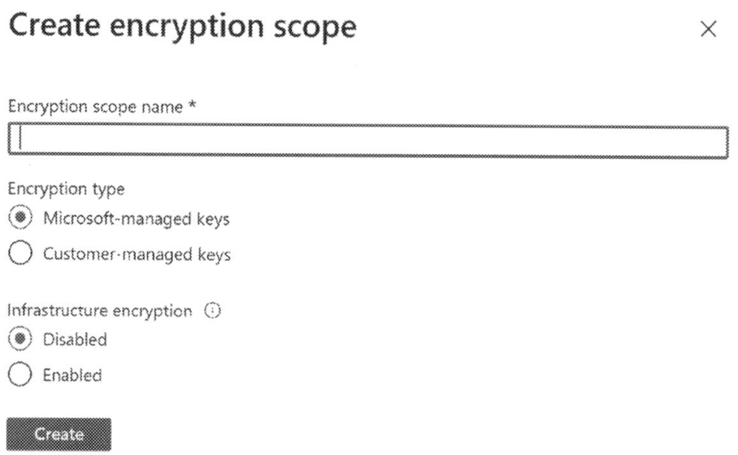

Figure 6-9. *Encryption scope*

We have discussed encryption mechanisms available with Azure storage in this lesson.

Lesson 6.3: Azure Defender for Azure Storage

Multilayer security practices are well-established and accurate mechanisms followed by many cloud providers. Security layers include physical and virtual security mechanisms. Security mechanisms enabling compliance add value to your organization's reputation. Azure storage has multilevel security features available.

There are several security threats introduced daily. New mechanisms to access systems in unauthorized ways are often found by hackers, terrorists, and other people stealing data. Azure storage users have to consider all these security threats available in the tech world and need to take all necessary steps to prevent cyber-attacks and enhance the security. Azure Defender is an intelligent security service that detects unusual and potentially harmful attempts to access or exploit the Azure storage accounts. It is a modern security alert system developed utilizing AI and Microsoft threat intelligence to provide security alerts and recommendations. Azure defender also sends details on security vulnerability to the administrators via email, and information on how to investigate the threat.

Azure defender identifies several activities as security threats and sends alerts. If there are unusual changes of access permissions, the defender identifies it and sends an alert. When trying to upload files and other content to storage that include malware files or phishing content, it will also alert the relevant users and administrator about the threat.

You can enable this feature from Azure security center. Go to Azure Security center and select pricing and settings from the side setting blade. Select Azure defender plans and enable the Azure defender for storage (see Figure 6-10).

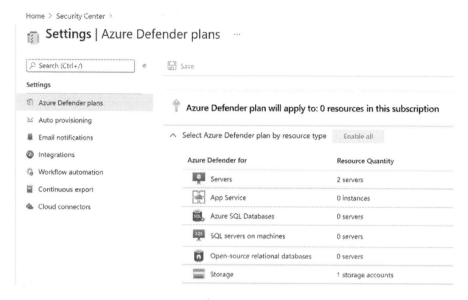

Figure 6-10. Defender

In this lesson we have discussed utilizing Azure defender for storage.

Summary

In this chapter we have discussed how to create Azure storage and how it can be utilized to save data securely. In the next chapter, you will learn about virtual networks.

CHAPTER 7

Ensuring Security Using Azure Virtual Networks

In modern software applications deployed in public clouds, security is essential because the nature of clouds poses a threat to your application deployed in cloud environments. Applying network-level security to the application deployed on PaaS service offerings as well as infrastructure on cloud are equally important. Azure comes with the concept of virtual networks, allowing you to have network layer protection to your applications. In this chapter let's explore a few aspects of virtual networks to understand how security for your applications can be implemented.

Lesson 7.1: Azure Virtual Networks and Subnets

You can create isolated and highly secured environments to run your applications and virtual machines using Azure virtual networks. Private IP addresses can be used to communicate within the virtual network, preventing outside traffic from entering except for the provided, configured, and secured options such as application gateways or load balancers.

© Pushpa Herath 2022
P. Herath, *Azure Cloud Security for Absolute Beginners*,
https://doi.org/10.1007/978-1-4842-7860-4_7

Azure virtual network ensures that the traffic flow between resources in a region does not use public Internet, but rather works with private Azure network. This makes communication from your virtual machines or app service apps reach storage or SQL instances in the network internally via Azure network, making such traffic exposed to public Internet and limiting the attacks. Using application firewalls and load balancers, you can effectively control traffic flows in between your Azure resources. You can also extend your corporate network to privately and securely connect to your Azure resources via virtual private network (VPN) or Azure express route, creating a bridge between your corporate network and Azure virtual network. Such implementation allows you to deploy your applications in hybrid topologies, where your web application in Azure may use SQL server instance deployed in your on-premise corporate network securely or authenticate with on-premise Active Directory.

Virtual networks further enable you to utilize PaaS and IaaS services together to run your applications. Web application roles can run PaaS App services, while your databases may be deployed to IaaS virtual machines and accessibility can be implemented with private Ips using virtual networks.

Additionally, you can use peering between virtual networks in Azure to allow secure communication of resources deployed in different virtual networks, even in different Azure subscriptions.

As we have already discussed the use of virtual networks, let's learn how to create a new virtual network as the next step.

As usual, begin by navigating to `https://portal.azure.com/` and logging in as an administrator.

Search for virtual networks and select Virtual network from the search result (see Figure 7-1).

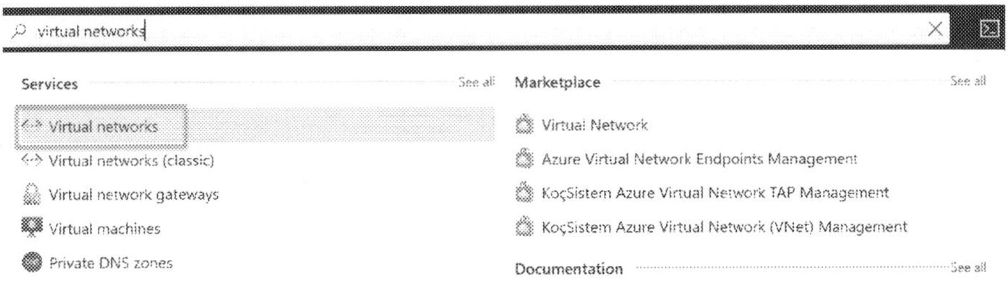

Figure 7-1. *Searching virtual network*

You will be navigated to the virtual network creation page. Click on the create button to start the creation process. You can select the relevant subscription, create or select a resource group for the vNet (virtual network), provide a name for the vNet, and select the region for the vNet (see Figure 7-2).

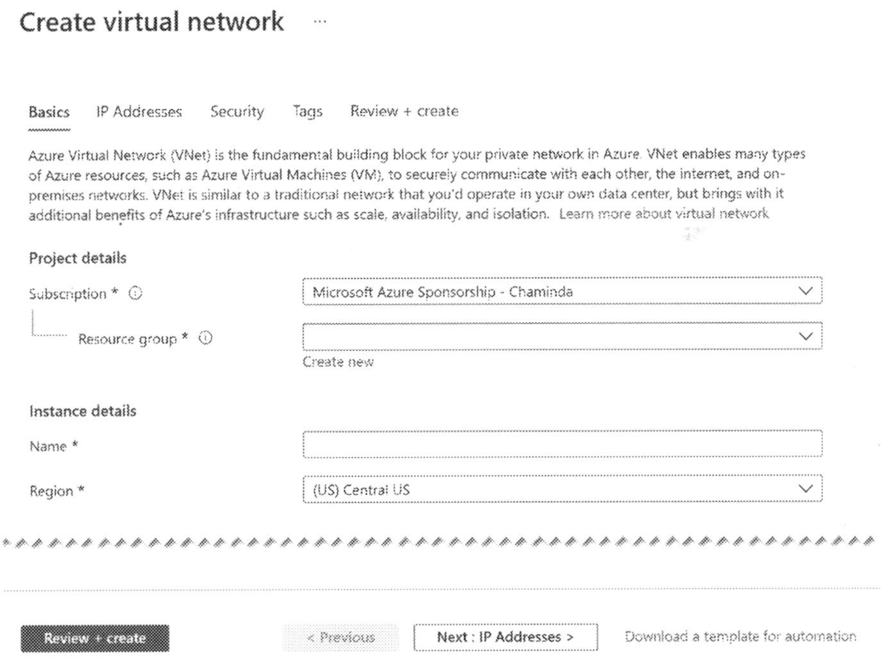

Figure 7-2. *vNet basic info*

Once basic information is added, go to IP Addresses. It is crucial to identify a suitable IP range for the virtual network; otherwise, it might give issues in the future when creating subnets and virtual network peering. Therefore, you need to properly design the network architecture for the organization before adding the IP range for the virtual network (see Figure 7-3).

Create virtual network ...

Basics   **IP Addresses**   Security   Tags   Review + create

The virtual network's address space, specified as one or more address prefixes in CIDR notation (e.g. 192.168.1.0/24).

IPv4 address space

| 10.1.0.0/16   10.1.0.0 - 10.1.255.255 (65536 addresses) | 🗑 |

| | |

☐ Add IPv6 address space ⓘ

The subnet's address range in CIDR notation (e.g. 192.168.1.0/24). It must be contained by the address space of the virtual network.

\+ Add subnet   🗑 Remove subnet

☐	Subnet name	Subnet address range	NAT gateway
☐	default	10.1.0.0/24	-

ⓘ Use of a NAT gateway is recommended for outbound internet access from a subnet. You can deploy a NAT gateway and assign it to a subnet after you create the virtual network. Learn more ☑

| Review + create | | < Previous | Next : Security > | Download a template for automation |

Figure 7-3. *vNet IP configuration*

IPv4 addresses: IPv4 addresses are 32-bit addresses. Provide IPv4 address with CIDR notation as a VNet address.

IPv6 addresses: You can select IPv6 address space, which allows you to create virtual networks that support both IPv4 and IPv6.

Subnet: Once the virtual network IP range is decided, you can add IP range for the subnets. It allows isolating the resources inside the virtual network into subnetworks. Such subnets are essential, as some Azure resources demand explicit delegations in a given subnet to be used to allow the resource to be associated with the subnet. For example, the web delegation "Microsoft.Web/serverFarms" is required to associate an app service app or function app to a virtual network. Such a delegated subnet may not be associated with other Azure resources depending on resource requirements in association with a subnet.

In the security tab you can do a few additional configurations to the virtual network (see Figure 7-4).

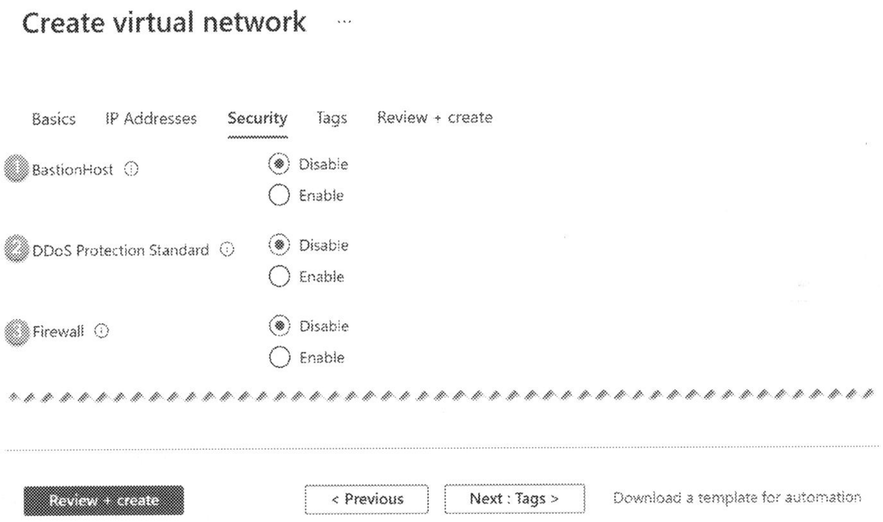

Create virtual network   ···

| Basics | IP Addresses | **Security** | Tags | Review + create |

BastionHost ⓘ
- ⦿ Disable
- ◯ Enable

DDoS Protection Standard ⓘ
- ⦿ Disable
- ◯ Enable

Firewall ⓘ
- ⦿ Disable
- ◯ Enable

Review + create   < Previous   Next : Tags >   Download a template for automation

Figure 7-4. Security of virtual network

BastionHost: Bastion is a mechanism that can be used to access virtual machines inside the virtual networks securely. It also allows access to the virtual machines remotely via browser without adding a Public IP to the virtual machine, which ensures that more secure virtual machines accessible to other resources only via private IP available on to the virtual network or to a peered network.

DDoS Protection Standard: Distributed denial of service attacks are well-known issues faced by the services that have endpoints that can be accessed through the public Internet. The nature of this attack is to exhaust an application resource and making the application unavailable to the legitimate users. The Azure DDoS protection feature provides adaptive tuning, attack notifications, and telemetry to protect resources inside the virtual network against DDoS attacks.

Firewall: This allows you to protect virtual networks by allowing access to virtual networks via dedicated firewall public IP. It allows only one entry point to the resources.

Once you provide the details, click on Review and create a button to create a virtual network and default subnet for it.

Let's understand a bit more about subnets in Azure virtual network. When you are creating a subnet in a virtual network, a couple of configurations can be made. The name of the subnet must be unique with the virtual network. The address space must be unique and should be within the address range of the virtual network. A network security group can be associated with the subnet specifying inbound and outbound traffic rules for the subnet. A route table can be associated with the subnet to specify routing s to other networks.

Service endpoints of a subnet lets you define the possible service associations to the subnet. For example, to associate a storage account with a subnet, service endpoint "Microsoft.Storage" should be added.

A subnet can be delegated to a given PaaS service, enabling the use of subnet for the given PaaS service type (see Figure 7-5).

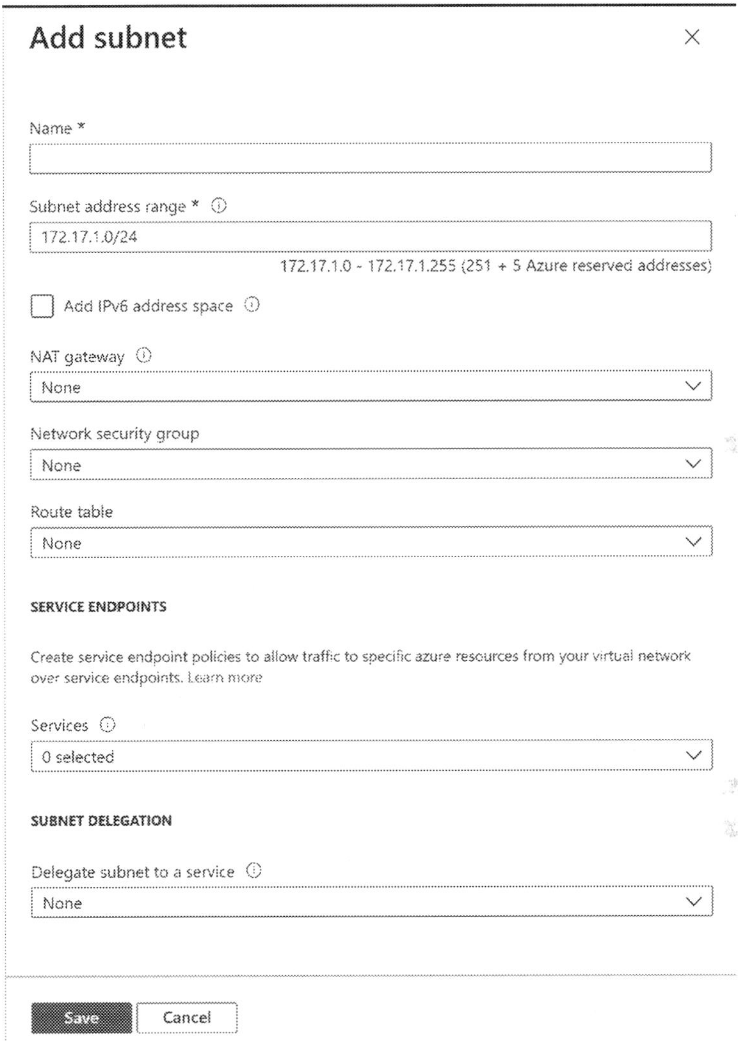

Add subnet   ✕

Name *

Subnet address range * ⓘ

172.17.1.0/24

172.17.1.0 - 172.17.1.255 (251 + 5 Azure reserved addresses)

☐ Add IPv6 address space ⓘ

NAT gateway ⓘ

None   ⌄

Network security group

None   ⌄

Route table

None   ⌄

SERVICE ENDPOINTS

Create service endpoint policies to allow traffic to specific azure resources from your virtual network over service endpoints. Learn more

Services ⓘ

0 selected   ⌄

SUBNET DELEGATION

Delegate subnet to a service ⓘ

None   ⌄

[Save] [Cancel]

Figure 7-5. *Creating subnet*

In this lesson we have discussed the use of virtual networks and subnets.

Lesson 7.2: Network Security Group

Virtual network is a good mechanism to protect the resources inside it. However, subnets can be defined inside virtual networks to group resources and protect them further. Once a resource is protected using a subnet, there should be an entry point to the resources inside. Azure network security groups are used to filter network traffic from and to the resources inside the VNet. Network security groups have rules that allow or deny the specific port to access the resources. More importantly, inbound and outbound network rules are controlled to several types of resources inside the network using network security groups. Optionally, you can associate a single NSG to all subnets in a virtual network and compartmentalize surety rules using application security groups across subnets based on application workloads as well, as we discussed in Chapter 5.

Let's learn how to create a network security group.

Go to https://portal.azure.com/ and log in as an administrator.

Search for Network security group and select Network security group from the search result (see Figure 7-6).

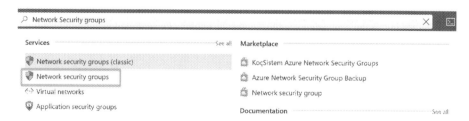

Figure 7-6. *Network security groups*

You will be navigated to the Network security group creation page. Click on the create button to start the creation process. Select subscription if there are multiple. Create a new resource group or select an existing resource group to save Network security group resources. Provide network security group name and select the region for the resource.

Once all the details are added, click on Review and the create button to create a network security group (see Figure 7-7).

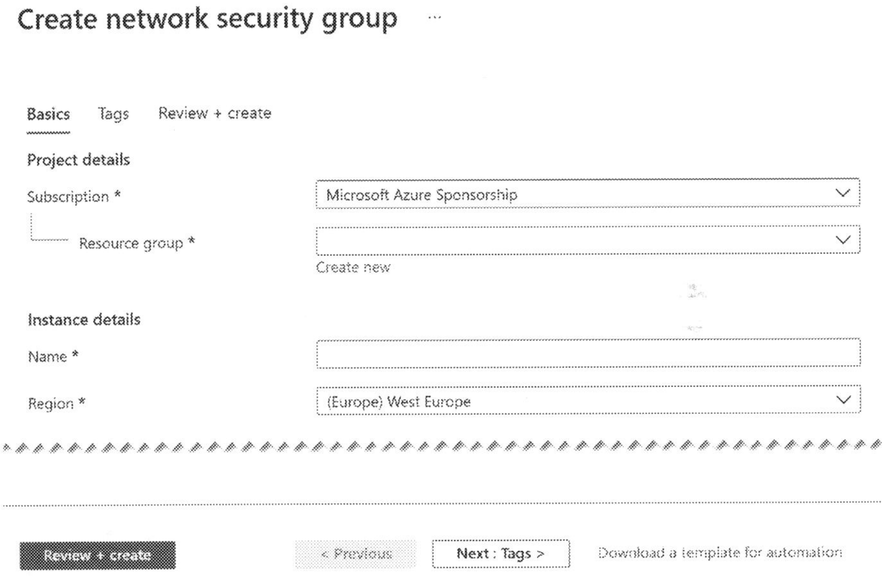

Create network security group   ...

Basics   Tags   Review + create

Project details

Subscription *	Microsoft Azure Sponsorship ⌄
⌐ Resource group *	⌄
	Create new

Instance details

Name *	
Region *	(Europe) West Europe ⌄

‹ ▰▰▰ ›

| Review + create | ‹ Previous | Next : Tags › | Download a template for automation |

Figure 7-7. Creating NSG

Go to the created network security group to add rules and associate subnets (see Figure 7-8).

145

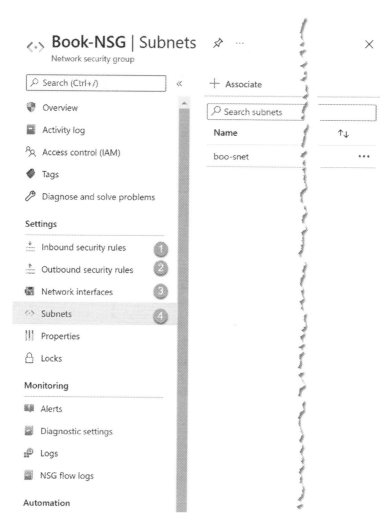

Figure 7-8. NSG

Inbound security rules: Inbound security rules are used to control the incoming traffic to the resource. This traffic can come from inside the Azure virtual network or from outside. Organizations can add inbound rules to allow or deny access to the resources from a specific IP range. This adds security and allows access only to the authorised services.

Outbound security rules: Outbound security rules are defined to allow or deny which ports can send data outside from the resources inside the virtual network.

Network interface: Network interface can be associated with a network security group. Network interfaces allow VMs to communicate with virtual networks or public Internet depending on settings.

Subnets: Subnetsare associated with NSG.

Let's see how we can use these network security groups in system architectures.

When designing the architecture for an application, there can be multiple servers used for different business needs such as hosting databases, handling web traffic, or handling business logic. These resources can be grouped in to subnets based on the architectural needs. However, grouping these resources using subnets does not give enough benefits until you control the network traffic accordingly. If you do not configure the security correctly, all the resources will be exposed to the public and virtual network. Basically, every resource can communicate with every other resource. This should not happen, as there are resources that should not be accessible from the public network and should even filter traffic from internal virtual networks. As a solution to such needs, network security groups can be used. We can use network security groups for each of the subnets. Then all the traffic coming through the public network has to go through the network security group to access the resources inside the subnet. You can define inbound and outbound rules to control the traffic of the subnet using Network security group to enable security of the resources inside the virtual network (see Figure 7-9).

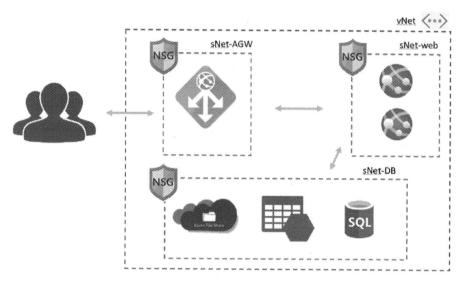

Figure 7-9. *Using subnets and NSGs*

An inbound rule generally defines which sort of inbound traffic is allowed. For example, take a remote desktop access rule applied for a VM. The remote port 3389 will be allowed with TCP protocol from any IP address to allow remote desktop access from public networks to the virtual machine (see Figure 7-10).

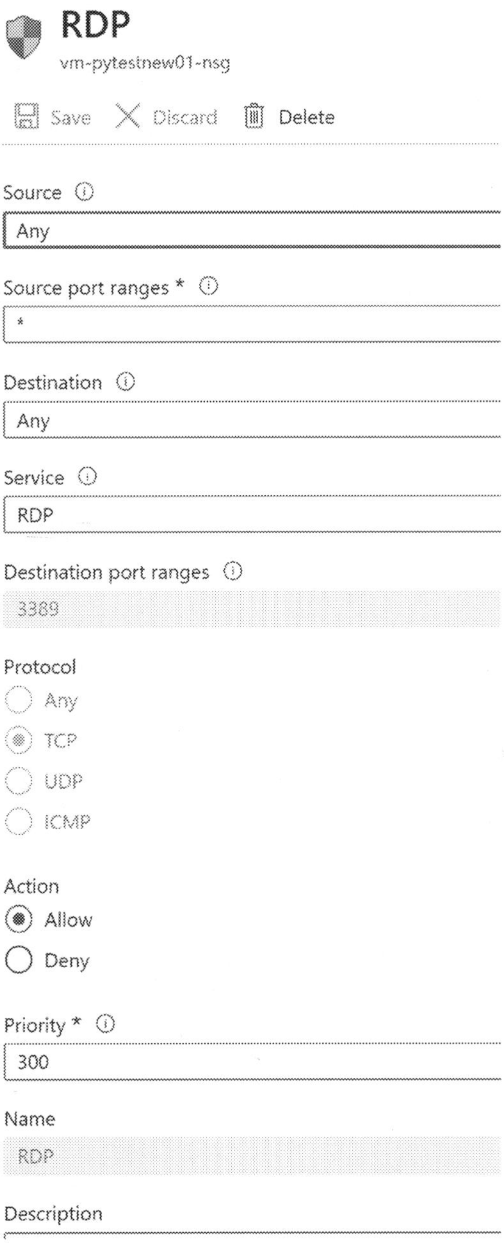

RDP

vm-pytestnew01-nsg

🖫 Save   ✕ Discard   🗑 Delete

Source ⓘ

Any

Source port ranges * ⓘ

*

Destination ⓘ

Any

Service ⓘ

RDP

Destination port ranges ⓘ

3389

Protocol

○ Any

◉ TCP

○ UDP

○ ICMP

Action

◉ Allow

○ Deny

Priority * ⓘ

300

Name

RDP

Description

Figure 7-10. *RDP rule*

Outbound rules are defined to control the traffic from resources to the outside of the subnet, or to the scope (can be application security group spanning across multiple subnets) applied by the NSG rule. For example, outbound traffic to Internet from resources can be allowed by setting the destination as Internet, as shown in Figure 7-11.

| Outbound security rules   ...

+ Add   ◌ Hide default rules   ⟳ Refresh   🗑 Delete   💬 Give feedback

Priority ↑	Name ↑↓	Port ↑↓	Protocol ↑↓	Source ↑↓	Destination ↑↓	Action ↑↓
65000	AllowVnetOutBound	Any	Any	VirtualNetwork	VirtualNetwork	✓ Allow
65001	AllowInternetOutBound	Any	Any	Any	Internet	✓ Allow
65500	DenyAllOutBound	Any	Any	Any	Any	✕ Deny

Figure 7-11.   Outbound rules

We have discussed how to create a network security group and use it to secure resources in Azure in this lesson.

Lesson 7.3: Azure VPN Gateways

Isolating the resources from the public access is one method of protecting the resources from unauthorized access from the public or other networks. However, entire isolation is not the best way of protecting data, as the services will be useless without enough required exposure to outside networks. VPN gateway is a network device that can be used as a solution. It can connect two or more virtual networks or devices. VPN devices can be routers, firewalls, or similar devices. Azure has a VPN service that creates bridges between virtual networks.

Let's see how to create a VPN gateway.

Go to https://portal.azure.com/ and log in as an administrator.

Search for Virtual network gateways and select Virtual network gateways from the search result (see Figure 7-12).

Figure 7-12. Virtual network gateways

You will be navigated to the Virtual network gateways creation page. Click on the create button to start the creation process (see Figure 7-13).

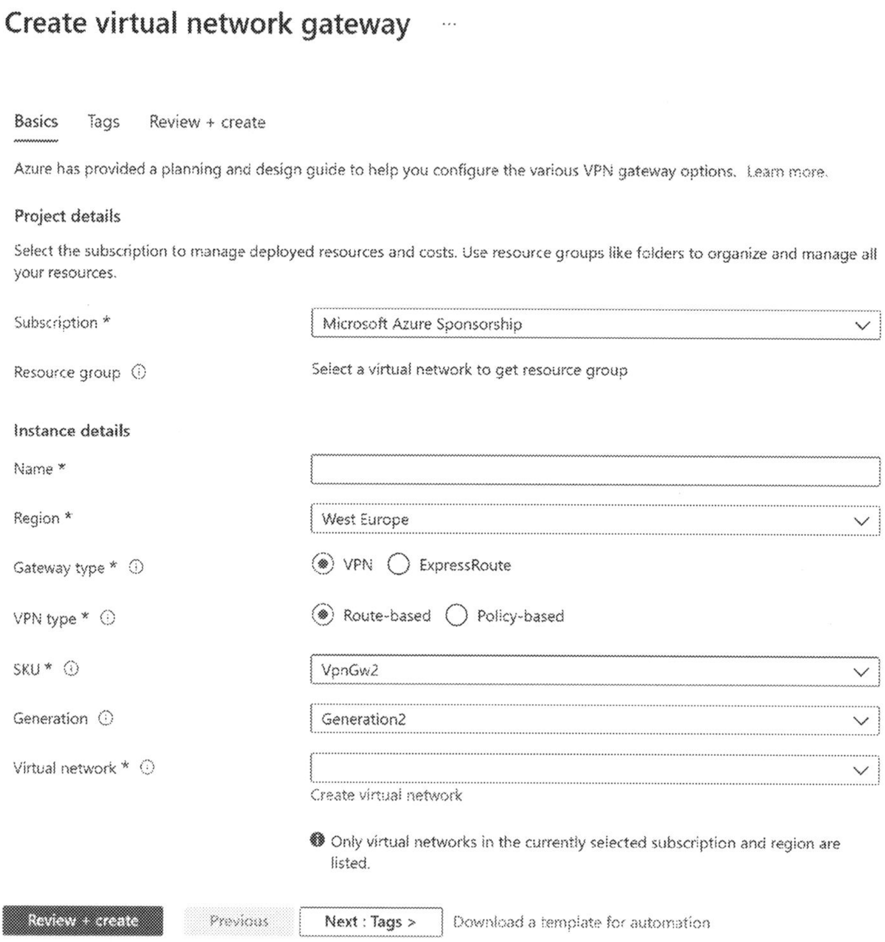

Create virtual network gateway   ...

Basics   Tags   Review + create

Azure has provided a planning and design guide to help you configure the various VPN gateway options. Learn more.

Project details

Select the subscription to manage deployed resources and costs. Use resource groups like folders to organize and manage all your resources.

Subscription *	Microsoft Azure Sponsorship ⌄
Resource group ⓘ	Select a virtual network to get resource group

Instance details

Name *	[ ]
Region *	West Europe ⌄
Gateway type * ⓘ	⦿ VPN ◯ ExpressRoute
VPN type * ⓘ	⦿ Route-based ◯ Policy-based
SKU * ⓘ	VpnGw2 ⌄
Generation ⓘ	Generation2 ⌄
Virtual network * ⓘ	[ ] ⌄
	Create virtual network

ⓘ Only virtual networks in the currently selected subscription and region are listed.

[Review + create]   Previous   [Next : Tags >]   Download a template for automation

Figure 7-13. *Creating virtual network gateway*

Select the relevant subscription if there are multiple. Virtual network gateway and virtual network should be in the same resource group. Once virtual network is selected, the same resource group will be added as the resource group of the VPN gateway.

Provide a proper name and select the region for the VPN gateway.

Gateway type can be VPN or ExpressRoute.

VPN: VPN gateway is used to send encrypted traffic across the public Internet. It is used to communicate between end points such as Site-to-Site, Point-to-Site, and VNet-to-VNet.

ExpressRoute: ExpressRoute is used to send network traffic on a private connection.

VPN type: Most of the time route-based VPNs are created to allow traffic to be determined based on routing/forwarding tables. Policy-based VPNs will use a combination of both networks' prefixes to define how the traffic is encrypted and decrypted. Policy-based are typically used in firewall devices.

SKU: SKU defines the feature availability and costing for your VPN.

Generation: This defines gateway SKU generation to be used based on the feature requirements and cost considerations.

Other than these details, you need to select the IP range for VPN gateway subnet.

Gateway needs a public IP to build up communication without virtual networks or devices, so add a new public IP or select an existing one. Also provide the public IP name and IP assignment type as Dynamic or Static (see Figure 7-14).

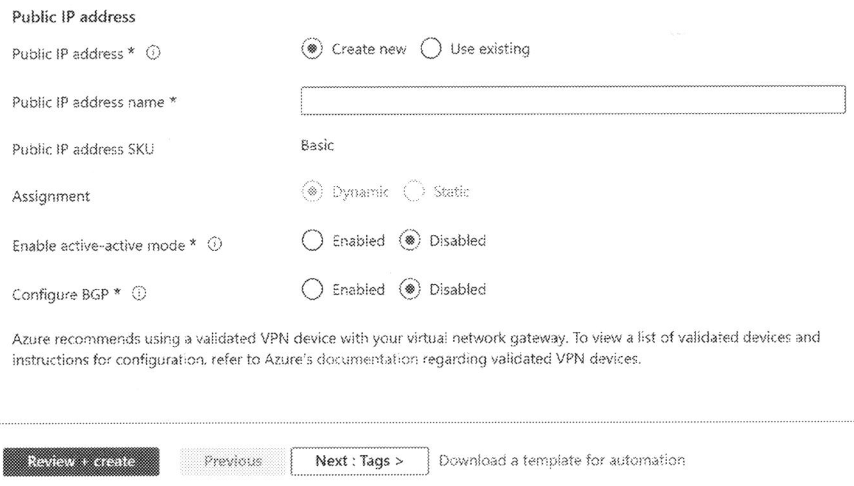

Figure 7-14. Gateway public IP

Enable active-active mode: Active-active mode allows you to create both instances of the gateway VMs to be connected with a tunnel to your on-premises VPN device.

Configure BGP: BGP is the standard routing protocol supporting exchange routing and reachability between two or more networks via the Internet.

You can now review and create your VPN gateway (see Figure 7-14).

Once you have your VPN gateway ready, which will take approximately 45 minutes, you can start configuring the gateway with the on-premise VPN device. Let's assume you are trying to create a site-to-site VPN connection. In this case, you need to have a local network gateway configured in Azure representing your on-premise location or the site.

When you are defining the local network gateway you need to specify the public IP of your on-premise device if you have a public static IP provided by your Internet service provider. Otherwise, you need to use a fully qualified domain name of your on-premise VPN device to enable connectivity to the local network gateway (see Figure 7-15).

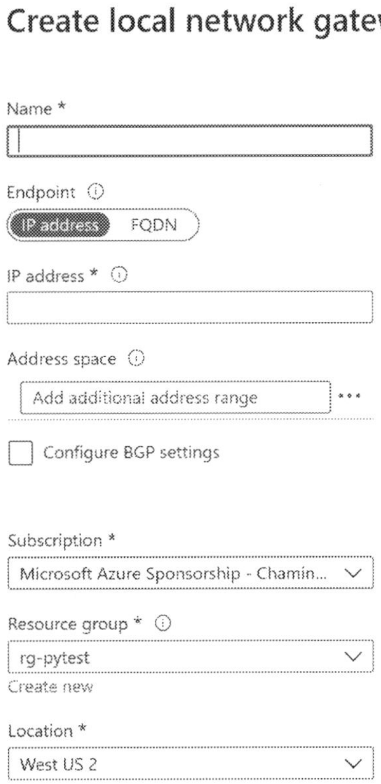

Create local network gateway

Name *

[   ]

Endpoint ⓘ
(**IP address**   FQDN)

IP address * ⓘ

[   ]

Address space ⓘ

[Add additional address range   ] •••

☐ Configure BGP settings

Subscription *

[Microsoft Azure Sponsorship - Chamin... ∨]

Resource group * ⓘ

[rg-pytest   ∨]
Create new

Location *

[West US 2   ∨]

Figure 7-15. *Local network gateway*

Configuring your local VPN device is the next step to enable the site-to-site VPN access. Depending on the VPN device you have in your on-premises network configuration, scripts can be downloaded from Azure virtual network gateway connection, which can be created inside your virtual network gateway. The connection will associate your Azure network gateway to your local network gateway (see Figure 7-16).

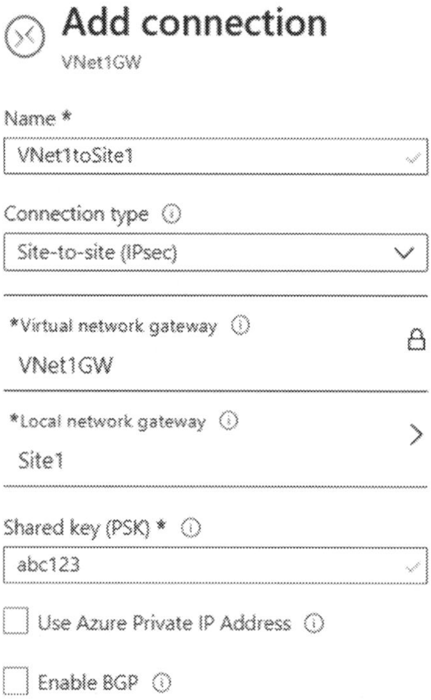

Figure 7-16. *Connection*

In the connection you can specify the local VPN device type and download the relevant scripts to configure your on-premise VPN device for site-to-site VPN access to your Azure network (see Figure 7-17).

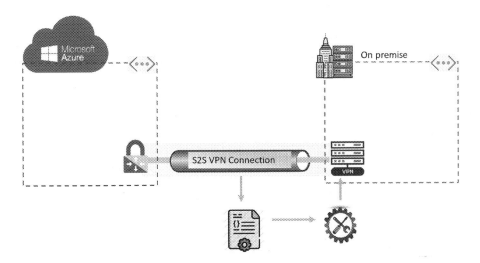

Figure 7-17. *Site-to-site VPN*

Configuring a VPN between your Azure virtual network and your on-premises network allows you to utilize hybrid deployment models for your applications. Your web applications may reside in Azure cloud while accessing some data from SQL servers in Azure, as well as on-premise SQL server deployed in a virtual machine in your corporate network securely without the threats from public Internet as connection between the two networks are private.

In this lesson, we have discussed setting up and using VPN gateways to enable secure access between on-premise corporate network resources and resources deployed in Azure.

Lesson 7.4: Azure Load Balancer

Load balancers are useful to evenly distribute incoming traffic to back-end servers or other resources such as web applications or function applications. Load balancer in Azure is considered as a single point of contact for the clients. The job of the load balancer is to distribute inbound flows arriving at the front end of the load balancer to back-end pool instances.

You can configure Azure load balancer as a public load balancer or as an internal load balancer. Internet traffic to your virtual machines can be load-balanced using a public load balancer, whereas internal load balancer would be used to load-balance internal traffic coming from within a virtual network.

Load balancer can manage internal and external traffic to Azure virtual machines. Load balancer can increase the availability of your back-end resources, because it can facilitate load balancing to resources deployed within and across zones. Health probes defined in load balancer help to monitor the back-end services' health continuously and ensure availability. Standard load balancers in Azure are secure by default, with a zero trust network model. NSGs can be used to define security rules to allow traffic explicitly in load balancer.

Let's explore how to create a load balancer.

Go to `https://portal.azure.com/` and log in as an administrator.

Search for Load balancers and select Load balancers from the search result (see Figure 7-18).

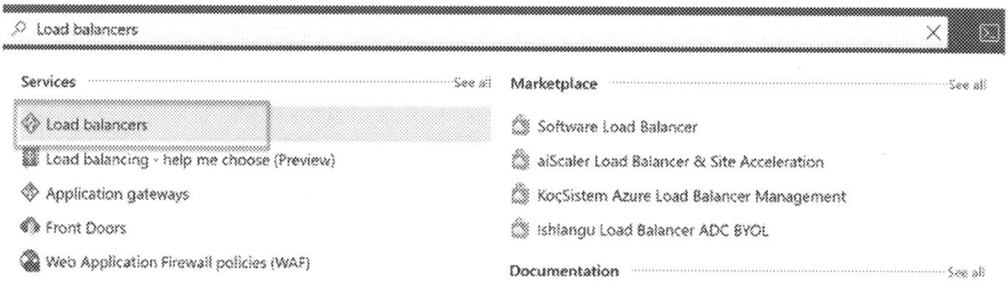

Figure 7-18. *Load balancers*

You will be navigated to the Load-balancers creation page. Click on the create button to start the creation process. You can select the Azure subscription and the resource group to add the load balancer. You can define a region to add the load balancer. The type of the load balancer can be defined as internal or public. Public load balancer will allow public network access to the load balancer. SKU can be defined to enable features at standard level, or you can use it as a basic load balancer. Basic load balancer is not recommended for the production workloads, as security enablement is less in basic. You can define the tier of the load balancer by region or as global. Global load balancing tier allows cross-region load balancing (see Figure 7-19).

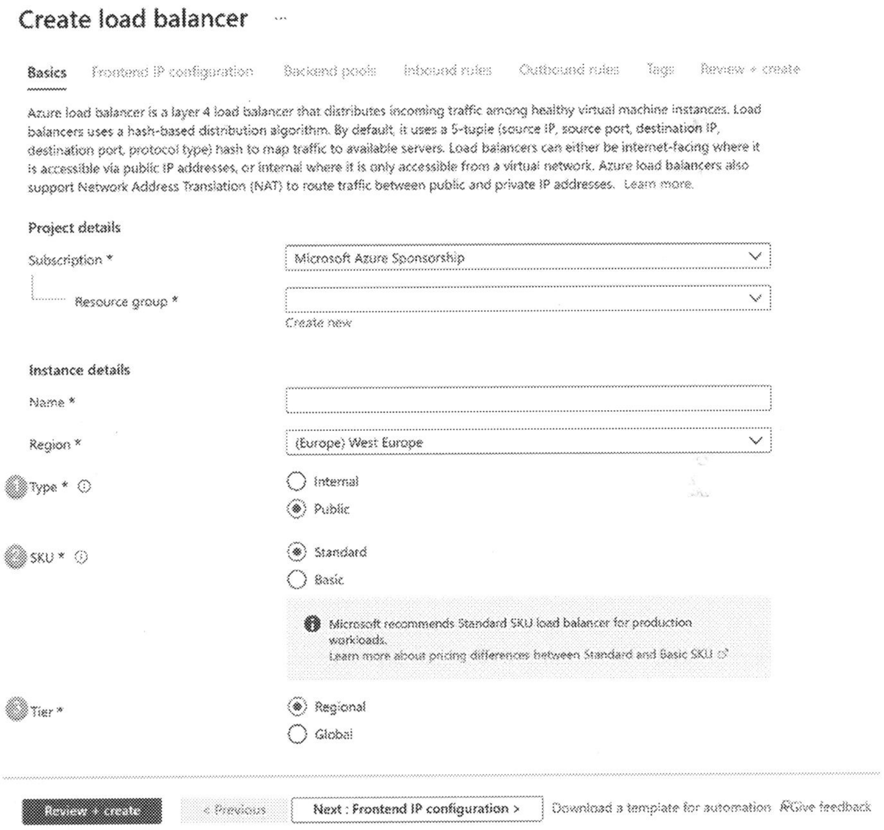

Figure 7-19. *Creating load balancer*

As the next step, you can define the front-end IP (see Figure 7-20).

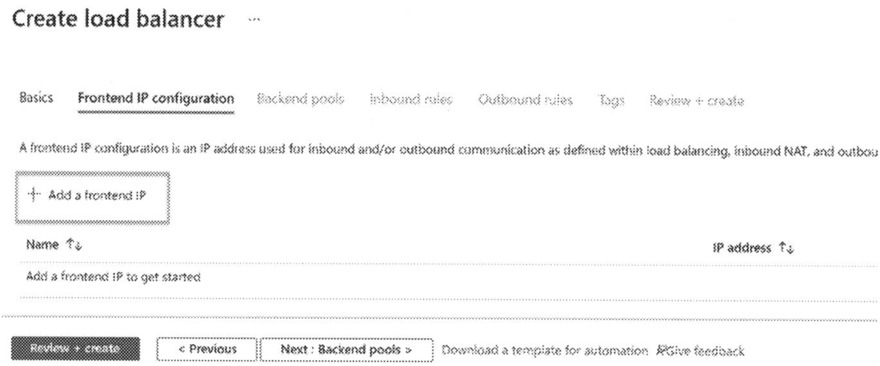

Create load balancer   ···

| Basics | **Frontend IP configuration** | Backend pools | Inbound rules | Outbound rules | Tags | Review + create |

A frontend IP configuration is an IP address used for inbound and/or outbound communication as defined within load balancing, inbound NAT, and outbou

+ Add a frontend IP

| Name ↑↓ | IP address ↑↓ |

Add a frontend IP to get started

| Review + create | | < Previous | | Next : Backend pools > | | Download a template for automation ♡Give feedback |

Figure 7-20. Adding front-end IP

If you are creating a public load balancer, you need to add a public IP to your load balancer as a front-end IP. You can set the IP version as IPv4 or IPv6. You can define IP and add an existing public IP or create a new public IP (see Figure 7-21).

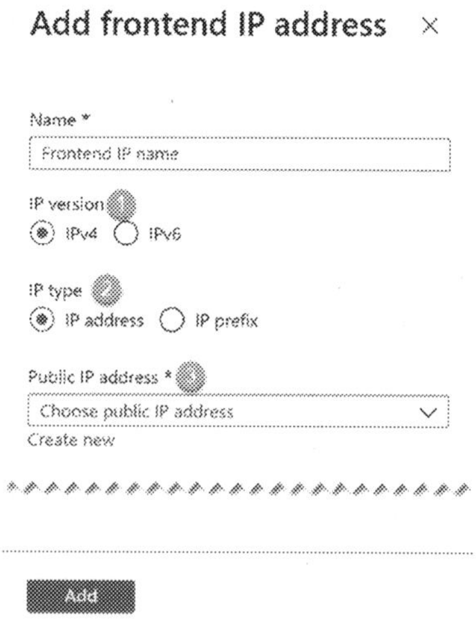

Add frontend IP address ✕

Name *

Frontend IP name

IP version

◉ IPv4 ◯ IPv6

IP type

◉ IP address ◯ IP prefix

Public IP address *

Choose public IP address   ⌄

Create new

Add

Figure 7-21. Adding public IP

The next step is to add the back-end pools for your load balancer. Click on add a back-end pool (see Figure 7-22).

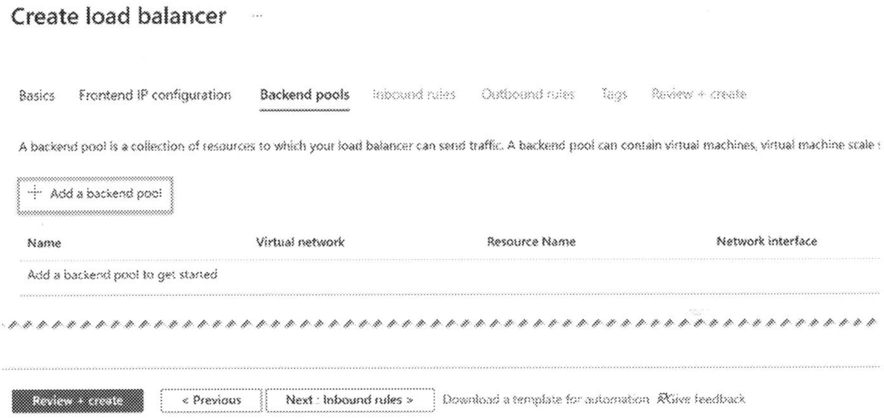

Figure 7-22. *Back-end pools*

You can define a back-end pool name and select a virtual network for your back-end pool. Then you can add the NIC or IP addresses of your back-end virtual machines (see Figure 7-23).

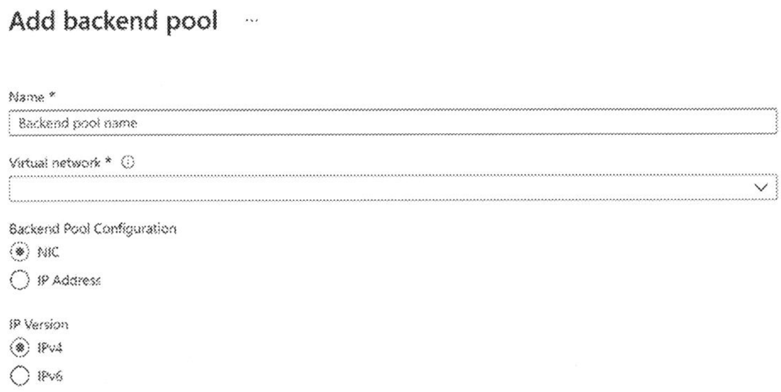

Figure 7-23. *Adding a back-end pool*

Next, you can add virtual machines or virtual machine scale sets to your load balancer (see Figure 7-24).

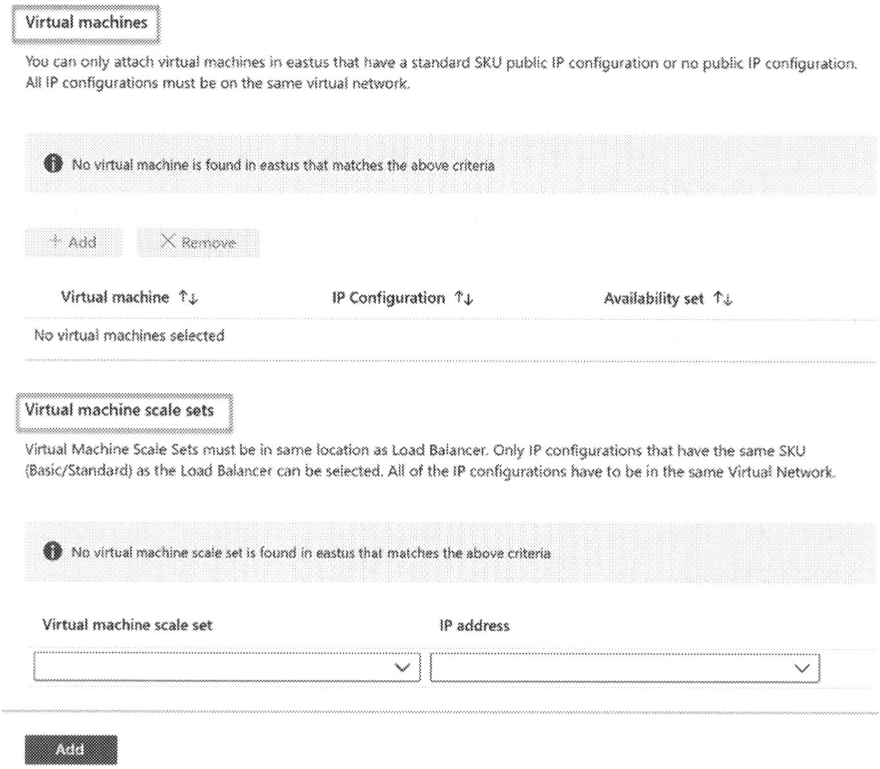

Figure 7-24. *Virtual machines and scale sets*

You can define load-balancing rules and inbound NAT rules to your load balancer. You can use the NAT rule when you have one back-end server to route incoming traffic, and when you have multiple back-end servers where incoming traffic should be load-balanced, you should use load-balancer inbound rules (see Figure 7-25).

Home > Load balancing - help me choose (Preview) >

Create load balancer ⋯ ⋯   ×

Basics   Frontend IP configuration   Backend pools   **Inbound rules**   Outbound rules   Tags   Review + create

Load balancing rule

A load balancing rule distributes incoming traffic that is sent to a selected IP address and port combination across a group of backend pool instances. The load balancing rule uses a health probe to determine which backend instances are eligible to receive traffic.

+ Add a load balancing rule

Name ↑↓	Frontend IP configu... ↑↓	Backend pool ↑↓	Health probe ↑↓	Frontend Port ↑↓	Backend port ↑↓
Add a rule to get started					

Inbound NAT rule

An inbound NAT rule forwards incoming traffic sent to a selected IP address and port combination to a specific virtual machine.

+ Add an inbound nat rule

Name ↑↓	Frontend IP configuration ↑↓	Service ↑↓	Target ↑↓	Frontend Port ↑↓
Add a rule to get started				

Review + create   < Previous   Next : Outbound rule >   Download a template for automation   Give feedback

Figure 7-25. Inbound rules

Outbound rules in a public standard load balancer allow you to define source network translation address (SNAT) rules where your back-end servers will be able to use public IPs of the load balancer to connect to the Internet (see Figure 7-26).

Create load balancer ⋯   ×

Basics   Frontend IP configuration   Backend pools   Inbound rules   **Outbound rules**

Outbound rules

An outbound rule allocates source network access translation (SNAT) ports from Frontend IP addresses to

+ Add an outbound rule

Name ↑↓	Frontend IP configuration ↑↓	Back
Add a rule to get started		

Figure 7-26. Outbound rules

Following these steps, you can create a load balancer in your virtual network.

Let's look at a simple implementation with load balancer to understand how to secure your applications' back-ends. You could use an internal load balancer to secure your back-end API servers where only internal network traffic from web servers in the virtual network is allowed to reach back-end APIs. A public-facing load balancer will control the flow of traffic to your web servers, further strengthening the security (see Figure 7-27).

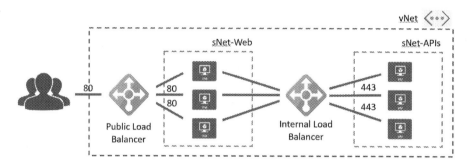

Figure 7-27. *Load-balancer use*

In this lesson, we have discussed setting up load balancer and different configuration options as well as how to implement secure networking to your resources.

Summary

In this chapter we have explored the virtual networks and subnets in Azure, allowing you to create private networks securing your PaaS and IaaS cloud resources. Use of network security groups to further strengthen the security via filtering traffic was discussed as well. The use of VPN gateways was explored to explain the possibility of secure private connections between your on-premise corporate networks and Azure cloud virtual networks. The Azure load balancer was discussed to understand the load balancing, as well as applying security to your back-end servers.

In the next chapter, let's explore more about Azure policies and security controls that can be applied to secure IaaS workloads.

CHAPTER 8

Azure Virtual Machine Security

Many systems use virtual machines-based solution architectures in the cloud to deploy the application workloads. Because Azure provides several ready-made virtual machine templates, such solutions in Azure are widely popular. However, deploying your application workloads into virtual machines requires you to manage security aspects by yourself to a greater extent than using PaaS services.

You need to protect your machines from viruses and malware, encrypt your sensitive data, create secure networking, identify and detect the threats to your data and applications deployed in virtual machines, and meet the required compliance policies. In order to implement such security requirements you need to take several steps, which we will be exploring in this chapter.

Lesson 8.1: Azure Security Center for VM Protection

Azure security center allows you to protect your infrastructure deployed in Azure in your datacenter or on-premise. Being an advanced and unified infrastructure security management system, Azure security center provides strengthened security of your data center.

© Pushpa Herath 2022
P. Herath, *Azure Cloud Security for Absolute Beginners*,
https://doi.org/10.1007/978-1-4842-7860-4_8

In IaaS in the Azure cloud, you have more responsibility for security compared to using PaaS services. You can utilize tools in Azure security center to harden your network and secure your services and infrastructure.

Before thinking about enhancing security, it is worth exploring what the security challenges in infrastructure deployed in Azure cloud are.

With cloud-based application workloads, having the option to change rapidly is considered a positive impact in the context of applications feature enhancements and productivity. However, such rapidly changing services raise the concern of whether the security standards required are always met or not. Failing to keep the security standard to required levels is a major concern in the rapidly changing nature of cloud-based application workloads.

As your cloud-based infrastructure is mostly the Internet, facing the risk of being attacked by more sophisticated attacks is higher. You need to ensure that you follow security best practices, or the vulnerability of your workloads will be much higher to be exposed to such attacks.

The scarcity of capable and skilled people to implement required security best practices is another issue in ensuring your cloud infrastructure security. Keeping your security stance current and ready for latest attacks is mandatory, and with less skilled resources, meeting such standards is challenging.

Azure security center strengthens your security posture by assessing your environment and providing information about your current security status. Providing threat prevention recommendations and alerts are also responsibilities of the security center. As a security center natively integrated to your cloud resources, it easily provides security to your Azure resources.

Azure security center works integrated with Azure defender to protect resources from threats. Azure Sentinel uses AI and manages and connects events occurring regarding security to trace down the related issues and threats to security in your environments (see Figure 8-1).

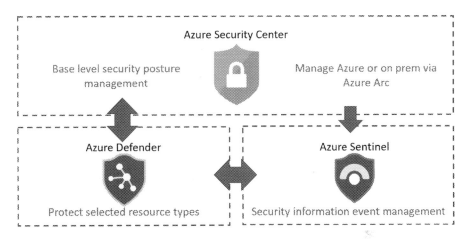

Figure 8-1. *Security center, defender, and sentinel*

Security Policy and Compliance

Azure security center policy controls are built on top of Azure policy controls, ensuring a fully flexible world-class security policy solution that is applicable across your subscriptions, management groups, and even for the entire tenant. You will be able to set up security policies via the security center. In the Security policy tab the subscriptions and management groups (if any) will be listed and you can select them to configure the security policies on them (see Figure 8-2).

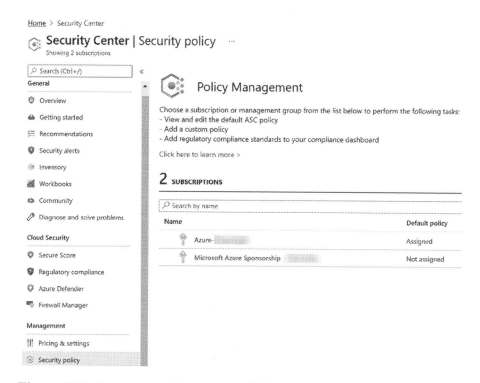

Figure 8-2. *Azure security center policies*

By clicking subscriptions or management groups, you will be able to apply policies to them (see Figure 8-3).

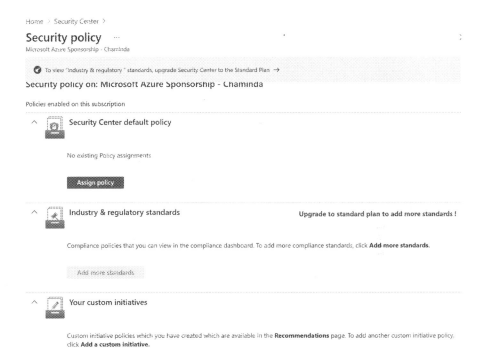

Figure 8-3. *Assign policies*

In Azure security center you will get a dashboard view for different perspectives of your subscriptions, management groups, and resources security. Secure score dashboard summarizes your current security state (see Figure 8-4).

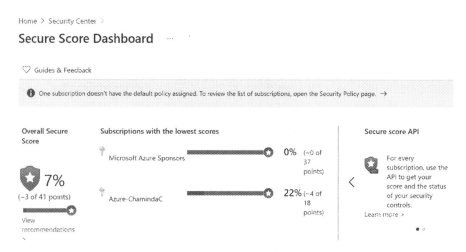

Figure 8-4. *Security score dashboard*

You will be able to view and even download reports on current security status and the recommendations depending on our resources' security state (see Figure 8-5).

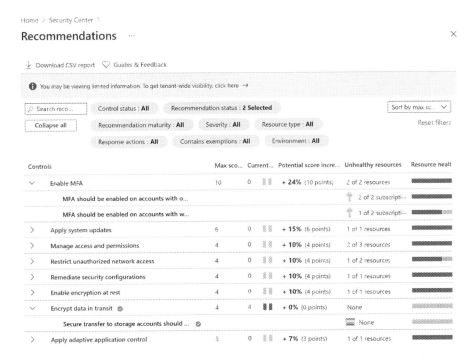

Figure 8-5. *Security recommendations*

In the recommendations, you might be able to execute a logic app to apply the remediation steps for a security concern (see Figure 8-6).

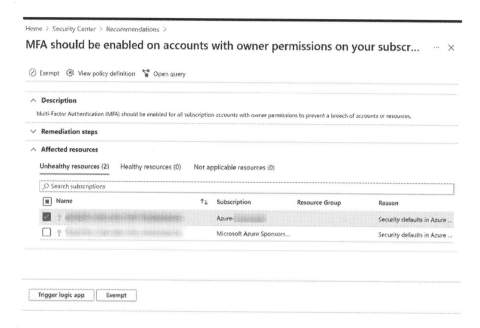

Figure 8-6. *Apply recommendation*

You can take manual steps recommended to apply the security policy
or exempt a resource from policy (see Figure 8-7).

Home > Security Center > Recommendations >

MFA should be enabled on accounts with owner permissions on your subscr...   ··· :

⊘ Exempt   ⊙ View policy definition   ⅍ Open query

⌄ **Description**

Multi-Factor Authentication (MFA) should be enabled for all subscription accounts with owner permissions to prevent a breach of accounts or resources.

⌄ **Remediation steps**

Manual remediation:

To enable MFA using conditional access you must have an Azure AD Premium license and have AD tenant admin permissions.

1 Select the relevant subscription or click 'Take action' if it's available. The list of user accounts without MFA appears.

2. Click 'Continue'. The Azure AD Conditional Access page appears.

3. In the Conditional Access page, add the list of users to a policy (create a policy if one doesn't exist).

4. For your conditional access policy, ensure the following:

  a In the 'Access controls' section, multi-factor authentication is granted.

  b. In the 'Cloud Apps or actions' section's 'Include' tab, check that Microsoft Azure Management (App Id :797f4846-ba00-4fd7-ba43-dac1f8f63013) or 'All apps' is selected. In the 'Exclude' tab, check that it is not excluded.

To enable MFA security defaults in Azure Active Directory (included in Azure AD free):

1. Sign in to the Azure AD - Properties page as a security administrator, Conditional Access administrator, or global administrator.

2. From the bottom of the page, select Manage security defaults.

3. Set Enable security defaults to Yes.

Figure 8-7. *Manual steps*

Security center regulatory compliance section will give you recommendations and details on actions required to make your resources compliance to the standards. The successful applied compliance policies, as well as failed policies, are indicated in detail for you to take actions (see Figure 8-8).

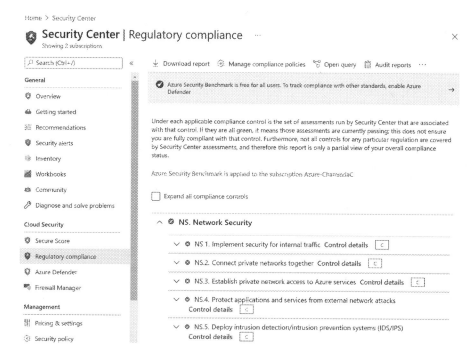

Figure 8-8. *Regulatory compliance*

Alerts section will provide with you the alerts on vulnerabilities exploited, and you can take necessary steps to remedy the issues (see Figure 8-9).

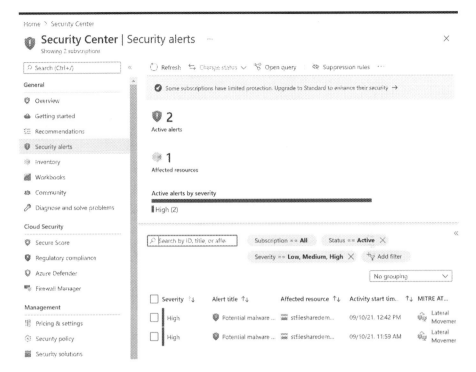

Figure 8-9. *Alerts*

As we have explored, there are many dashboards and tooling available with Azure security center enabling you to secure your resources deployed in Azure.

In this lesson we explored Azure security center to understand how it can help to improve the security posture of our cloud deployed workloads.

Lesson 8.2: Availability for Azure VMs

The idea of making your cloud resources available to your customers and employees with unhindered access at any time from anywhere is important. Such availability requires you to consider how you should deploy your infrastructure in the cloud.

In this lesson, let's look at options and features in Azure to make your virtual machines highly available.

Availability Set

Logical grouping of virtual machines is called an availability set. In an availability set you can expect availability and redundancy for your applications deployed into the virtual machines. You don't have to pay extra to use an availability set; however, the virtual machine instances created in the availability set will be charged depending on the virtual machine size. A fault domain can be considered as a rack of servers. If one of the virtual machines fails, another having the same role from a fault domain can serve the application needs, as they are in sync (see Figure 8-10).

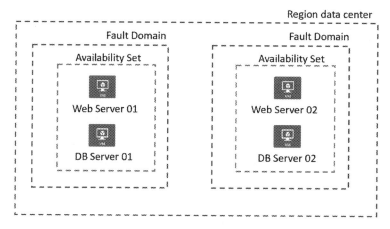

Figure 8-10. *Availability sets*

Availability Zones

Within an Azure region, physically separated zones allowing separate physical hardware, networking power, and cooling are provided to ensure that one zone failure does not affect the other. In a supported Azure region, there are three availability zones where you can replicate your virtual machine. If a zone fails, replication of apps and data will be immediately available in another zone (see Figure 8-11).

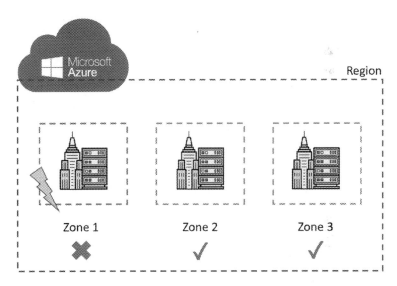

Figure 8-11. *Availability zones*

Virtual Machine Scale Sets

You can create a managed group of virtual machines that are load-balanced using Azure virtual machine scale set. You can set the number of virtual machines in the scale set to be increased or decreased as per the demand of requests or as per a schedule. Scale set facilitates to centrally manage and deploy your application workloads in a scalable and reliable manner with a single set of configurations. The scale set itself will not cost you, but the virtual machine instances running at a given time will add to the cost.

Utilizing the previously mentioned Azure features with relevant load-balancing options will provide your applications with high availability and resiliency. To ensure the security of your application data, the availability of your applications play an important role because it will minimize the data corruptions that may occur in highly distributed and decoupled modern solutions if availability is compromised.

We have discussed the availability options in Azure for virtual machines in this lesson.

Lesson 8.3: Azure Bastion

Keeping your virtual machines with the highest possible level of controlled exposure to public access is vital to ensure the security of applications and data deployed to such machines. Therefore, deploying your virtual machines with only private IPs and enabling access only via the virtual network is an essential security consideration. See Figure 8-12 for example scenario.

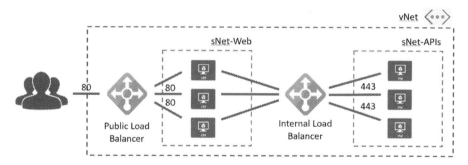

Figure 8-12. *Secure deployment of application*

In a scenario where your virtual machines are secured with a virtual network and only assigned with private IPs, the applications will be exposed to the public via load balancers or application gateways as appropriate. However, you might have to access these virtual machines for administrative purposes. In such situations, since you do not have a public IP assigned to the virtual machine, it is not possible to access the virtual machine unless you create a jump box (another virtual machine with a public IP) in the same virtual network.

As an alternative to creating an additional virtual machine as a jump box, Azure now offers Bastion as a service where you can use it to access the virtual machines deployed only with private Ip using your browser securely. Azure bastion lets you RDP/SSH into your virtual machines securely using the private IP of the virtual machine. Bastion service is deployed to a subnet in the virtual network and the Internet access is provided to bastion service and you can use Azure portal to access your virtual machines over TLS (transport layer security) (see Figure 8-13).

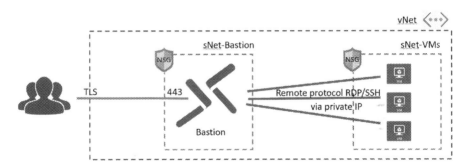

Figure 8-13. Bastion

Let's look at steps in deploying a bastion service to securely access a virtual machine with only private IP. We can get started with creating a virtual machine in Azure with only private IP and without opening any ports for public RDP (see Figure 8-14).

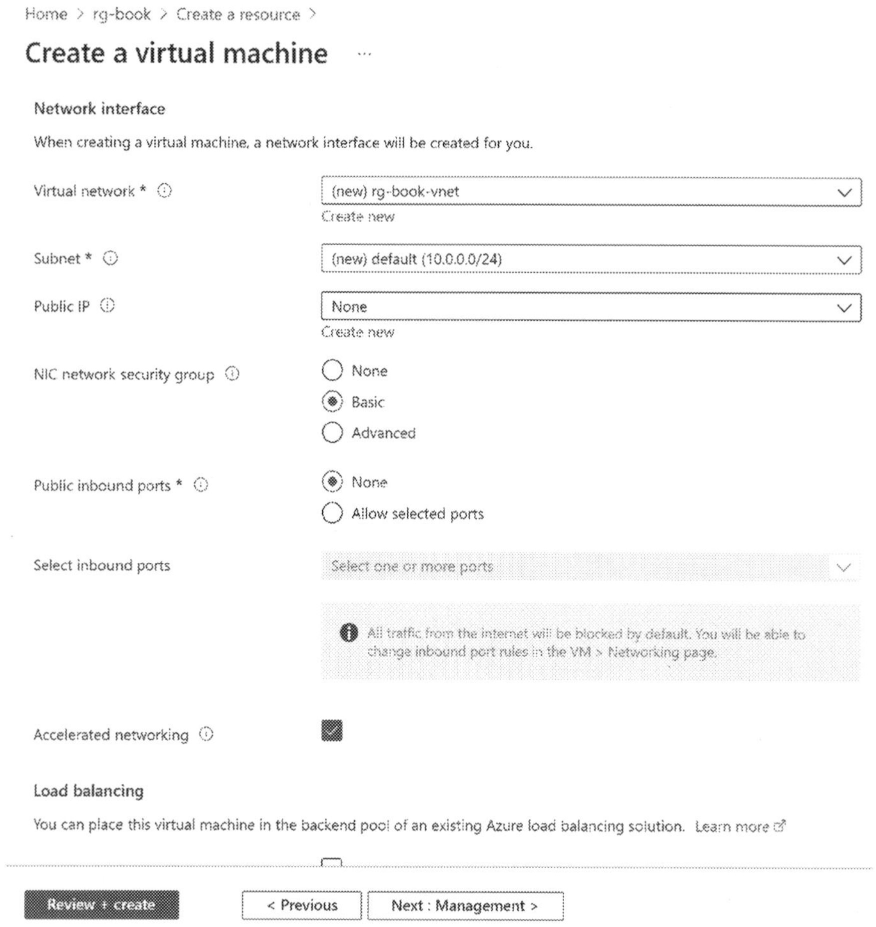

Create a virtual machine   ...

Network interface

When creating a virtual machine, a network interface will be created for you.

Virtual network * ⓘ	(new) rg-book-vnet ⌄
	Create new
Subnet * ⓘ	(new) default (10.0.0.0/24) ⌄
Public IP ⓘ	None ⌄
	Create new
NIC network security group ⓘ	◯ None
	◉ Basic
	◯ Advanced
Public inbound ports * ⓘ	◉ None
	◯ Allow selected ports
Select inbound ports	Select one or more ports ⌄

> ⓘ All traffic from the internet will be blocked by default. You will be able to change inbound port rules in the VM > Networking page.

Accelerated networking ⓘ	☑

Load balancing

You can place this virtual machine in the backend pool of an existing Azure load balancing solution. Learn more ⧉

Review + create   < Previous   Next : Management >

Figure 8-14. *VM with no public IP and RDP port*

Once the virtual machine is created, you can click on the connection in the Azure portal in the virtual machine overview page and click Bastion. Notice that there is no public IP for the virtual machine (see Figure 8-15).

Figure 8-15. Connect VM

Next, you need to click the Use Bastion button to deploy the bastion service to the virtual network (see Figure 8-16).

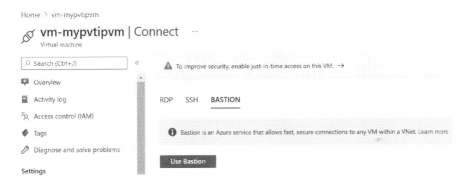

Figure 8-16. Use Bastion

You will see a create the subnet for bastion, as is prompted. Optionally, you can use a network security group as well with the subnet to enable more secure deployment (see Figure 8-17).

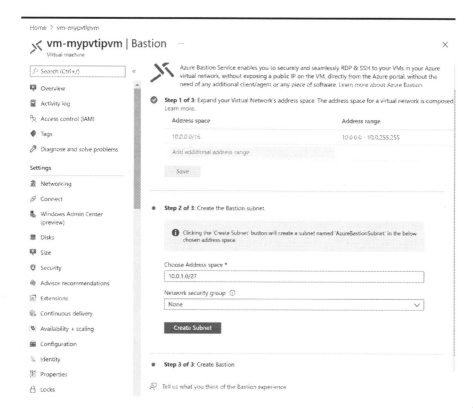

Figure 8-17. *Subnet for bastion*

Next, you can create the bastion service providing the name of your preference. A public IP for the bastion service will be created as well (see Figure 8-18).

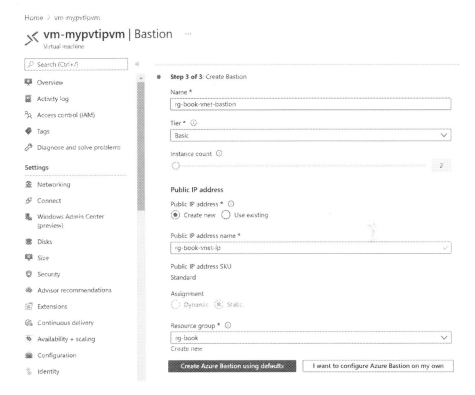

Figure 8-18. *Create bastion*

Once bastion is deployed in your virtual network you can connect the virtual machine by just providing the user's name and the password for RDP access (see Figure 8-19).

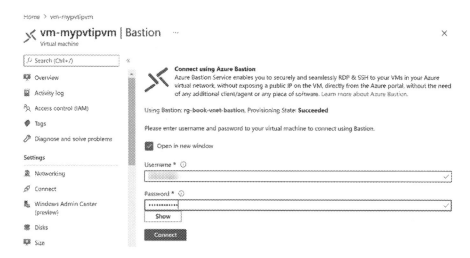

Figure 8-19.   *Connect VM via bastion*

You will RDP into the virtual machine with the browser via bastion (see Figure 8-20).

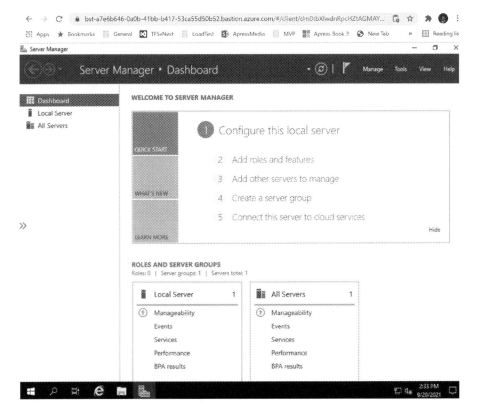

Figure 8-20. *RDP via bastion*

Any other virtual machines in the same virtual network can be accessed via the bastion service you deployed in the virtual network. The access to the virtual machine is limited via the Azure portal and to the people you have specifically granted access in identity and access management controls in Azure, ensuring the security of your virtual machines as opposed to virtual machines exposed with a public IP to the Internet and opening up RDP or SSH port publicly.

In this lesson we have discussed how to securely access virtual machines with only private IPs and without any RDP/SSH port opening, utilizing bastion service via Azure portal.

Summary

In this chapter we have explored the Azure security center to understand the security policy enforcement over the resources deployed in Azure, and monitoring, alerting, and providing recommended configurations for secure deployment of resources. We have also discussed available deployment options enabling application and data security. Additionally, administrative access to securely via Azure portal with bastion service was described to further enhance your knowledge of security of infrastructure in Azure.

In the next chapter, we are going to discuss the use of firewalls in Azure to secure resources.

CHAPTER 9

Securing Resources with Azure Firewall

Cloud resources need to be protected against growing cyber threats. Therefore, it is required that you take proactive security implementations to ensure the safety of the resources deployed. Network security is a fundamental security aspect you need to have in place to strengthen the security of your resources. Azure offers you a firewall where you can manage and control the traffic to your resources from the Internet and from your resources to the Internet. While different types Azure firewalls perform different functions within the Microsoft cloud, they predominantly act as monitors for interactions between a given section of the public cloud and the rest of the Internet. By filtering packets and requests, these firewalls can block malicious software from getting access to applications, data, or even the network itself. The Microsoft Azure Marketplace sells firewalls that generally fall into two categories: Web Application Firewalls and Network Firewalls. The firewall we are discussing in this chapter is the network firewall.

© Pushpa Herath 2022
P. Herath, *Azure Cloud Security for Absolute Beginners*,
https://doi.org/10.1007/978-1-4842-7860-4_9

Lesson 9.1: Setting Up Azure Firewall

Azure firewall enables you to secure your virtual network and the resources in the virtual network. You can define various rules and policies in a firewall. To begin with, let's understand how to deploy a firewall in Azure.

Go to `https://portal.azure.com` and log in as an administrator.

Search for firewall and select firewall from the search results (see Figure 9-1).

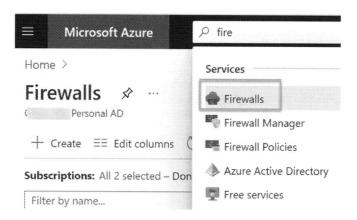

Figure 9-1. *Searching for firewall*

Click on the create button to start the firewall creation process (see Figure 9-2).

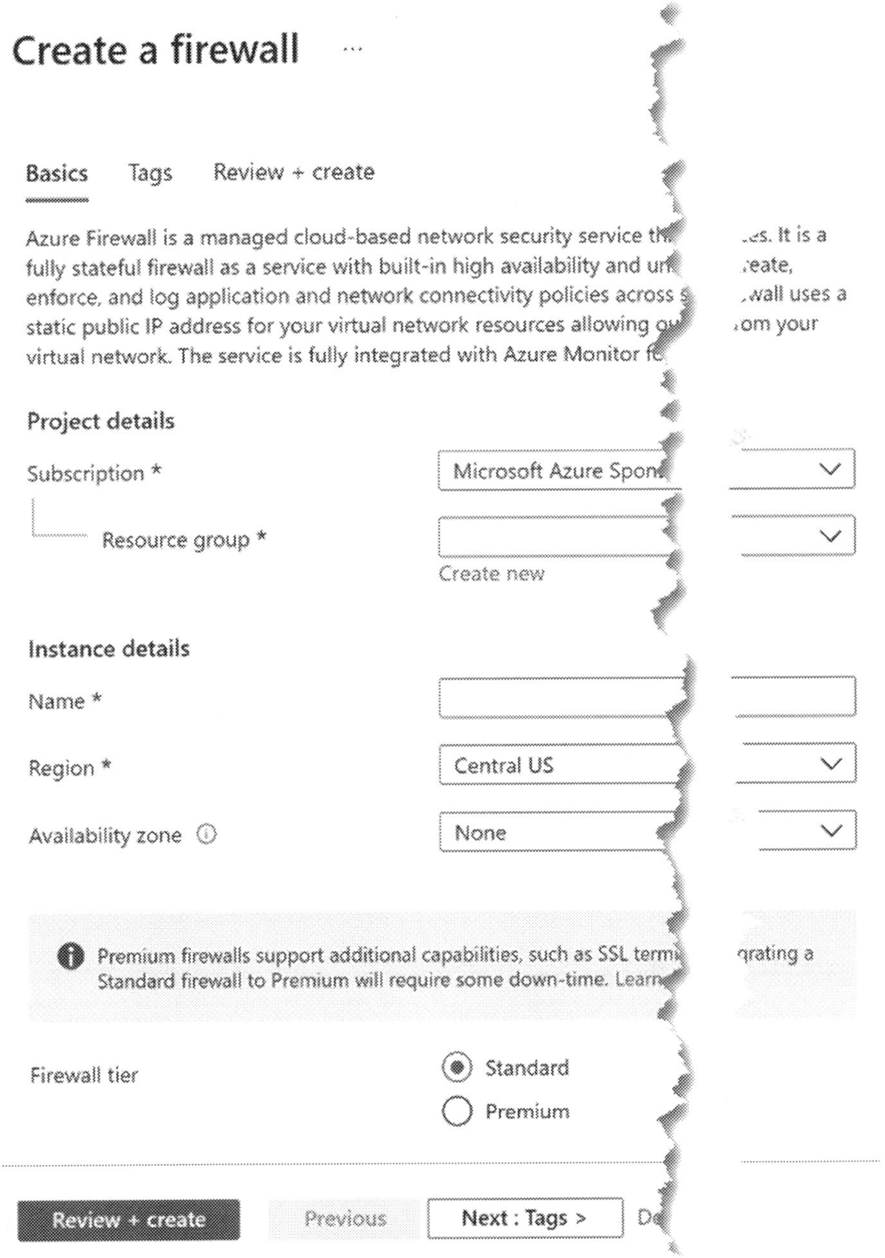

Create a firewall ...

Basics   Tags   Review + create

Azure Firewall is a managed cloud-based network security service th   ..s. It is a
fully stateful firewall as a service with built-in high availability and un   .eate,
enforce, and log application and network connectivity policies across   ,wall uses a
static public IP address for your virtual network resources allowing o   .om your
virtual network. The service is fully integrated with Azure Monitor f

Project details

Subscription *   Microsoft Azure Spon

Resource group *

Create new

Instance details

Name *

Region *   Central US

Availability zone ⓘ   None

ⓘ Premium firewalls support additional capabilities, such as SSL term   qrating a
Standard firewall to Premium will require some down-time. Learn

Firewall tier   ⦿ Standard
                             ○ Premium

Review + create   Previous   Next : Tags >   De

***Figure 9-2.** Firewall basic info*

Select subscription if there are multiple subscriptions. Create a new resource group or select an existing resource group to maintain resources of the firewall.

Enter a name for the firewall and region of the firewall.

To increase the availability 99.99% for your firewall, you can deploy it to availability zones in Azure.

While creating an Azure firewall you need to set up a couple of configuration values, as shown in Figure 9-3.

Figure 9-3. *Firewall information*

1: Firewall tier: Firewall tiers have two versions: standard and premium. Standard is the version of firewall supporting older features such as classic firewall rules. You can use standard policy management as well.

Premium is a more advanced and newer version of firewall with enhanced security features. You cannot use classic rules in premium. However, you can choose to use standard or premium policies.

2: Firewall management: You can select firewall policies or classic firewall rules to manage the firewall. You will learn more about these in the next lesson of this chapter. This option is only selectable when using standard firewall tier. Premium firewall tier will always use the firewall policies to manage the firewall.

3: Firewall policy: For standard firewall tier you can only select policy tier standard. For premium firewall tier you can select either premium or standard firewall (see Figure 9-4).

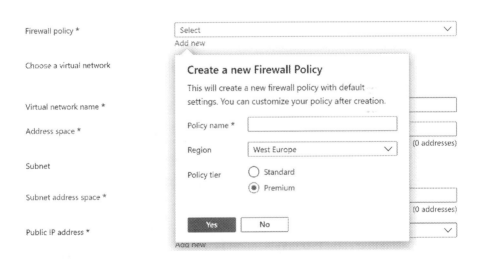

Figure 9-4. *Firewall policy*

4: Choose virtual network: You can select existing virtual network or create new virtual network for the firewall.

5: Virtual network name: Provide the name of the virtual network and select the address range for the firewall subnet. Keep in mind that Azure firewall subnet should be named as AzureFirewallSubnet; you are not allowed to choose a different name for the firewall subnet.

9: Public IP address: Public IP is one of the main features of Azure firewall. You need to open a port to route the traffic from outside to the virtual network. This public IP of the firewall is used for all the incoming traffic to the virtual network.

10: Forces tunneling: You can configure a new firewall to route Internet-bound traffic to a designated hop without going directly to the public Internet.

We have discussed how to create an Azure firewall. Let's learn more about firewall features and capabilities.

TLS inspection: Transport Layer Security (TLS) protocol facilitates the communication of an application across networks in a secure manner ensuring confidentiality and integrity of the communications. TLS inspection consists of server and client protection. Client protection inspects the outgoing traffic from the protected network where server protection inspects the incoming traffic. Azure firewall decrypts outbound traffic, processes the data, and then encrypts the data and sends it to the destination and takes care of client TLS inspection (see Figure 9-5). Inbound/server TLS inspection is supported with Azure application gateway, providing end-to-end encryption.

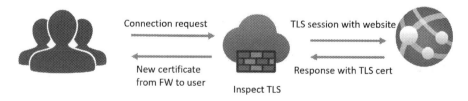

Figure 9-5. TLLS Inspection

IDPS: The network intrusion detection and prevention system (IDPS) monitors the network activities to detect, log, and report malicious activities, and attempts to block such activity. Signature-based IDPS in Azure firewall helps to detect the attacks rapidly, and IDPS can monitor both inbound and outbound traffic.

URL filtering: Azure firewall has filtering capability extending to entire URL filtering with FQDN filtering. URL filtering helps you to prevent users from accessing URLs that are not work-related, potentially harmful, or objectionable.

Web categories: Based on categorizations, you can prevent access to web sites for your users with web categories capability. Such setup will allow you to prevent users from accessing websites promoting inappropriate content such as alcohol, child abuse, criminal activities, gambling, and so on.

Category exceptions: You can filter certain categories of websites from being accessed while allowing a site in the same category specifically with the category exceptions. For example, if all other social media platforms such as Facebook and Instagram are blocked, you can specifically allow LinkedIn access to your employees because of the professional nature of the site.

In this lesson we have discussed setting up an Azure firewall and its features in brief. Let's explore the Azure firewall further in the next lessons.

Lesson 9.2: Azure Firewall Policies

In terms of the security of data and applications, it is important to control who can access data and applications from the outside. It is equally important to control outgoing traffic from the organization's network, which is the outbound traffic. There may also be situations where organizations need to limit the access to the specific websites from the organization's network, such as gaming sites or even social media sites, which affect employee productivity on a large scale. Azure policies can be used to control the access to public Internet from the organization's network.

Azure firewall policy consists of network, network address translation (NAT), application rules, and threat intelligence system. You can apply policies across subscriptions and regions using Azure firewalls. You can create a firewall policy from scratch or inherit one from an existing policy and extend it to create your policy. While your firewall can be in any subscription associated with your account and in any region, it can be utilized with policies in other subscriptions and other virtual networks. Such capability allows you to set up a base set of policies for the organization that can be inherited to create specific policies for given applications. Parent policy rules will be inherited to the policy created as inherited policy in firewall (see Figure 9-6).

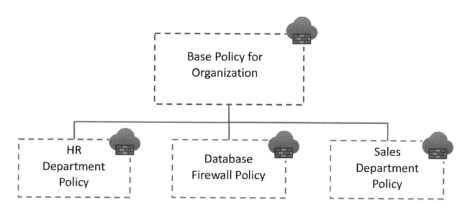

Figure 9-6. *Policy inheritance*

The priority goes to network rules collection in parent policy, and then the specified network rules in the child policy get evaluated. The same priority applies to the application rules. However, all network rules are processed before processing any application rules. For example, consider the rules specification shown in Figure 9-7.

Base Policy for Organization
App Rule 1 – Priority 100
Net Rule 1 – Priority 300
HR Department Policy
App Rule 2 – Priority 101
Net Rule 2 – Priority 303
Database Firewall Policy
App Rule 3 – Priority 104
Net Rule 3 – Priority 301
Sales Department Policy
App Rule 4 – Priority 102
Net Rule 4 – Priority 302

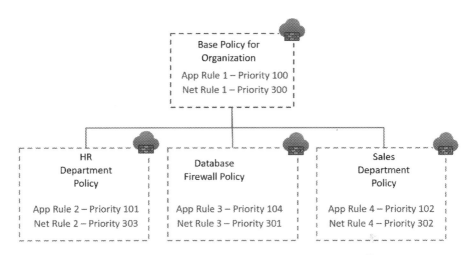

Figure 9-7. *Rule specification*

The rules specified in policies, as in Figure 9-7, will be executed in the order shown in Figure 9-8.

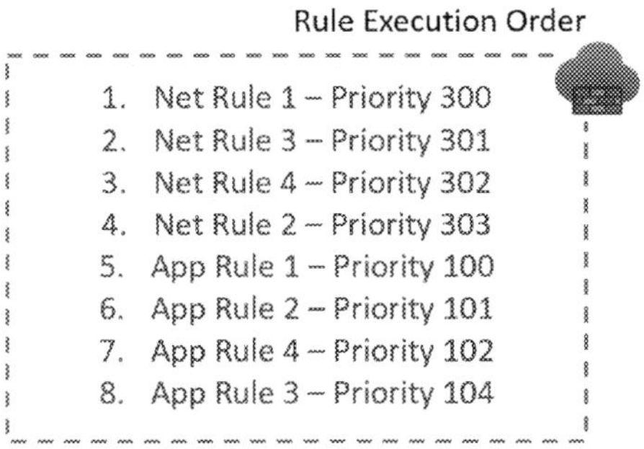

Rule Execution Order
1. Net Rule 1 – Priority 300
2. Net Rule 3 – Priority 301
3. Net Rule 4 – Priority 302
4. Net Rule 2 – Priority 303
5. App Rule 1 – Priority 100
6. App Rule 2 – Priority 101
7. App Rule 4 – Priority 102
8. App Rule 3 – Priority 104

Figure 9-8. *Execution order*

Rules are processed in a terminating way; that is, if a matching rule is found in execution order, then no other rules are processed.

In a firewall you can find the policy in the overview page, as shown in Figure 9-9.

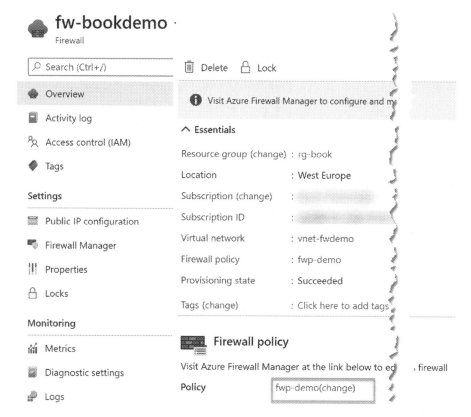

Figure 9-9. *Policy manager*

In the policy you can set up network and application rules. You can also inherit from the policies defined in other subscription firewalls (see Figure 9-10).

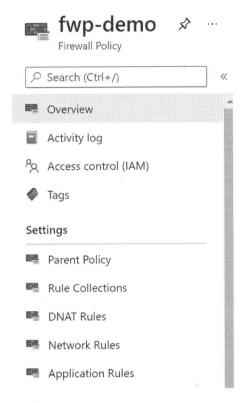

Figure 9-10. Firewall policy

DNAT or destination network address translation can be used to translate and filter inbound Internet traffic to your resources in the virtual network protected by the firewall. When adding DNAT rules it is recommended that you use a specific Internet source without using wildcards to ensure security. Network rules and application will control the outbound connectivity, while DNAT rules control the inbound connectivity.

Rule Collection

A rule collection can be of type network, application, or DNAT. You can set a priority to a rule collection, and a collection can contain multiple rules of the same type (see Figure 9-11).

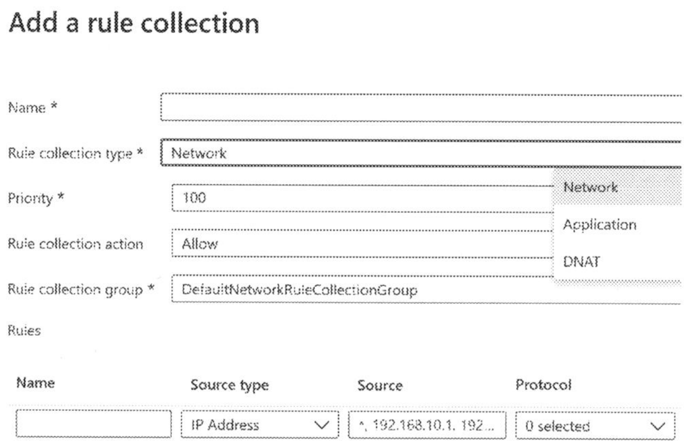

Add a rule collection

Name *	
Rule collection type *	Network
Priority *	100
Rule collection action	Allow
Rule collection group *	DefaultNetworkRuleCollectionGroup

Network
Application
DNAT

Rules

Name	Source type	Source	Protocol
	IP Address ∨	*, 192.168.10.1, 192 …	0 selected ∨

Figure 9-11. *Rule collection*

Rule Collection Group

A single rule collection group can contain multiple rule collections of different types where rules in a single rule collection must be of the same type (network, application, or DNAT). Rules are processed based on rule collection group priority. See Figure 9-12 to understand how a rule collection group can be created with a name and priority.

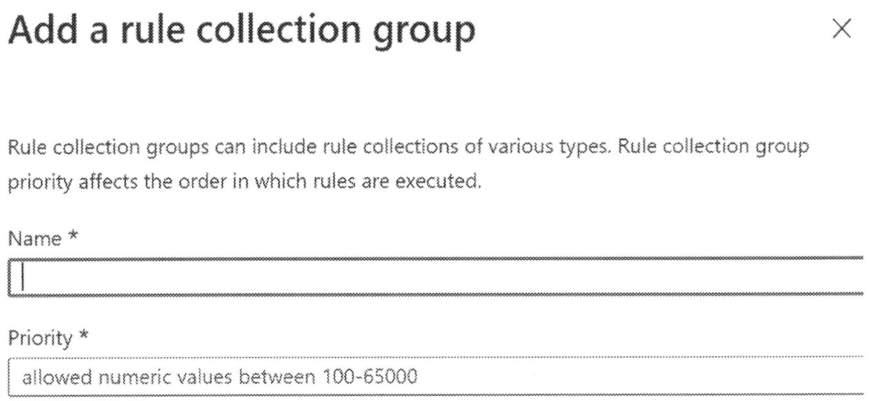

Add a rule collection group   ✕

Rule collection groups can include rule collections of various types. Rule collection group priority affects the order in which rules are executed.

Name *

[   ]

Priority *

[allowed numeric values between 100-65000   ]

Figure 9-12. *Rule collection group*

If your firewall policy has been inherited from a parent policy, the priority is always given to the rule collection groups in the parent policy, regardless of individual rule collection priority setting in child policy. However, DNAT rules are processed first, network rules second, and application rules third in the order regardless of policy inheritance, rule collection priority, or rule collection group priority. In other words, rule policy inheritance, rule collection group priority, rule collection priority, and rule priority are respected with one type of rule (DNAT, network, or application).

Threat Intelligence

Threat intelligence helps to alert and prevent traffic to and from malicious domains or IPs. Microsoft threat intelligence feed will provide the domains and IPs that are known as malicious. When threat intelligence is enabled in your firewall policy it gives precedence to any of the DNAT, network, or application rules in your firewall policy. Allowed list lets you define domains or IPs that should be allowed without filtering. See Figure 9-13 for more information.

🖫 Save   ⟳ Refresh

Parent policy: None

Threat intelligence

Threat intelligence based filtering can be enabled for your f̲ ͩwn
malicious IP addresses and domains. The IP addresses and ҉   .at
Intelligence feed. You can choose between three settings: ｛

- **Off** - This feature will not be enabled for your firewall ｝
- **Alert only** - You will receive high confidence alerts for ｛   known
  malicious IP addresses and domains
- **Alert and deny** - Traffic will be blocked and you will re̪   mting to
  go through your firewall to or from known malicious IP ad̠

Learn more about threat intelligence

Threat intelligence mode ⓘ | Alert Only   ｝ ⌄ |

Allow list addresses

Threat intelligence will not filter traffic to any of the IP add̪   ,
whether contained in uploaded files, pasted, or typed indiv̪

＋ Add allow list addresses

IP address, range, or subnet	Inherited from ｛
*, 192.168.10.1, or 192.168.10.0/24	

Fqdns

Fqdn	Inherited from ⤟
* or *.microsoft.com or *azure.com	

Figure 9-13. *Threat intelligence*

Azure firewall policy is an ideal way to define the rules for the firewall to ensure protection of the resources you deploy in Azure, as described in this lesson.

Lesson 9.3: Azure Firewall Manager

Azure firewall manager is a service available in Azure allowing you to manage security policies and routes in a central security management service. Secured virtual hubs where you can create hub or spoke architecture in Azure virtual wide area network hub, which is managed by Microsoft, is one of the architecture types that can be managed with firewall manager. The other is the standard Azure virtual network, also called a hub virtual network, which you should manage and create.

Azure firewall manager helps you to centrally deploy Azure firewalls and manage them. These firewalls can be in different subscriptions in different regions.

Hierarchical global and local policies can be managed with firewall manager, and global firewall policies allow you to define organization wide policies (see Figure 9-14).

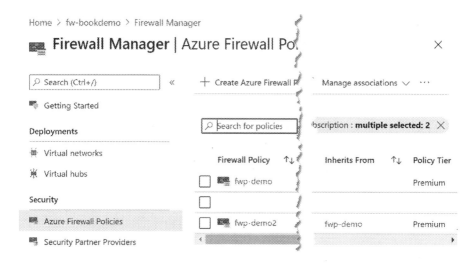

Figure 9-14. Firewall policies

From firewall manager you can create secured virtual networks, and you can see the virtual networks in your subscription with information about whether the firewall policy applied or not (see Figure 9-15).

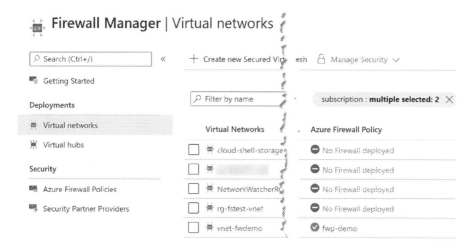

Figure 9-15. Firewall manager vNets

Managing firewall policies can be assigned to global or local administrators based on requirements of the organization or relevant departments. Global policies can be managed and applied by the global admins and local hub virtual network or secure WAN (wide area network) hub policies managed by respective local administrators (see Figure 9-16).

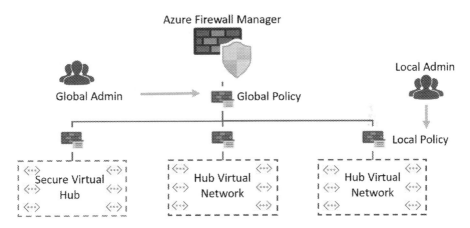

Figure 9-16. *Managing policies*

Azure firewall manager allows you to effectively manage complex environments created with different network architectures that adopt the Hub and Spoke model over Azure Virtual WAN (wide area network). The firewall management service is an essential tool to manage firewall policies and routes more easily and effectively in the Azure network architecture, and will be getting more features sooner.

Summary

In this chapter, we have discussed Azure firewall in detail to understand the capabilities and use of firewall to secure your applications by applying firewall policies and rules.

In the next chapter, we will discuss isolated and secured implementation of app services with app service environments.

CHAPTER 10

App Service Environments

Implementing security in some applications requires full isolation from other resources. Azure app service environments (ASE) provide a dedicated fully isolated environment to deploy Windows and Linux web apps, docker containers, and function apps. Essentially, app service apps can run in full isolation, with isolated higher network security and access, high scalability, high memory utilization, and catering for higher requests per second, in an app service environment.

App service environment deployed apps are already in a virtual network without you having to do any additional configurations. Your ASE is a single tenant system that is not shared with anyone else providing isolation fully to your apps. You can even demand that your ASE be deployed into dedicated hardware to have complete isolation.

Version 3 of ASE supports creating up to 200 app service plans, and version 2 supports up to 100 plans. Apps in ASE can access resources in the virtual network of the ASE without you having to perform any additional configurations. With ASE version 3 you can deploy as a zone redundant as well.

© Pushpa Herath 2022
P. Herath, *Azure Cloud Security for Absolute Beginners*,
https://doi.org/10.1007/978-1-4842-7860-4_10

Lesson 10.1: Setting Up Azure App Service Environment

With the brief understanding we have about app service environments (ASEs), let's get started by setting up an ASE.

In Azure portal you can search for app service environments (see Figure 10-1).

Figure 10-1. *Searching for ASEs*

You can click on Add to get started, creating your first ASE (see Figure 10-2).

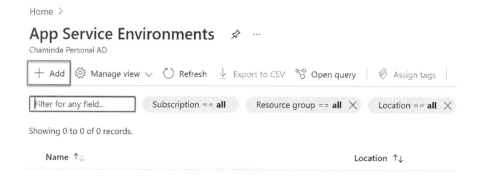

Figure 10-2. *Adding ASE*

In the basic information page of ASE, select an existing resource group or provide a name to create a new resource group. A name for ASE should be provided. You can select the virtual IP of ASE to be internal, which would create it as an internal load-balancer endpoint (see Figure 10-3).

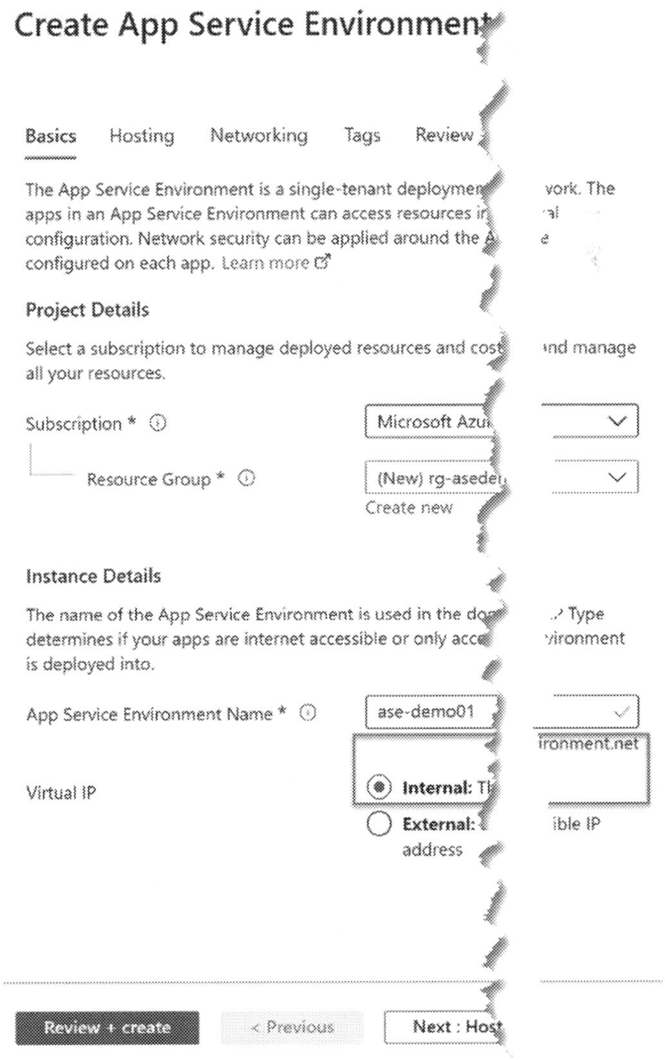

Create App Service Environment

Basics   Hosting   Networking   Tags   Review

The App Service Environment is a single-tenant deploymen̶   vork. The apps in an App Service Environment can access resources i̶   ̶al̶ configuration. Network security can be applied around the A̶   ̶e̶ configured on each app. Learn more ✂

Project Details

Select a subscription to manage deployed resources and cost̶   ̶nd manage all your resources.

Subscription * ⓘ	Microsoft Azu̶	∨
Resource Group * ⓘ	(New) rg-asede̶	∨
	Create new	

Instance Details

The name of the App Service Environment is used in the do̶   ̶ Type determines if your apps are internet accessible or only acc̶   ̶vironment is deployed into.

App Service Environment Name * ⓘ	ase-demo01	∨
		ironment.net
Virtual IP	⦿ **Internal:** T̶	
	◯ **External:** ̶ ̶ble IP	
	address	

Review + create   < Previous   Next : Hos̶

Figure 10-3. Creating ASE basics

If you switch virtual IP to external, notice the change in address of the ASE suffix (see Figure 10-4). Let's proceed with External for virtual IP.

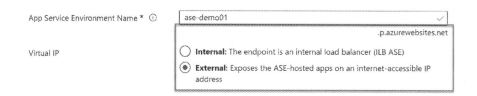

Figure 10-4. *External virtual IP*

In the hosting page, you can select to deploy the ASE to dedicated hosts. Normally ASE is deployed on VMs, which are provisioned on multitenant hypervisors. If you choose to enable dedicated hosts it will deploy on dedicated hardware. However, zone redundancy would not be available for dedicated hosts, and dedicated hosts always be deployed as a pair to ensure redundancy. While deploying the ASE in normal mode you can choose to deploy as a zone redundant (see Figure 10-5).

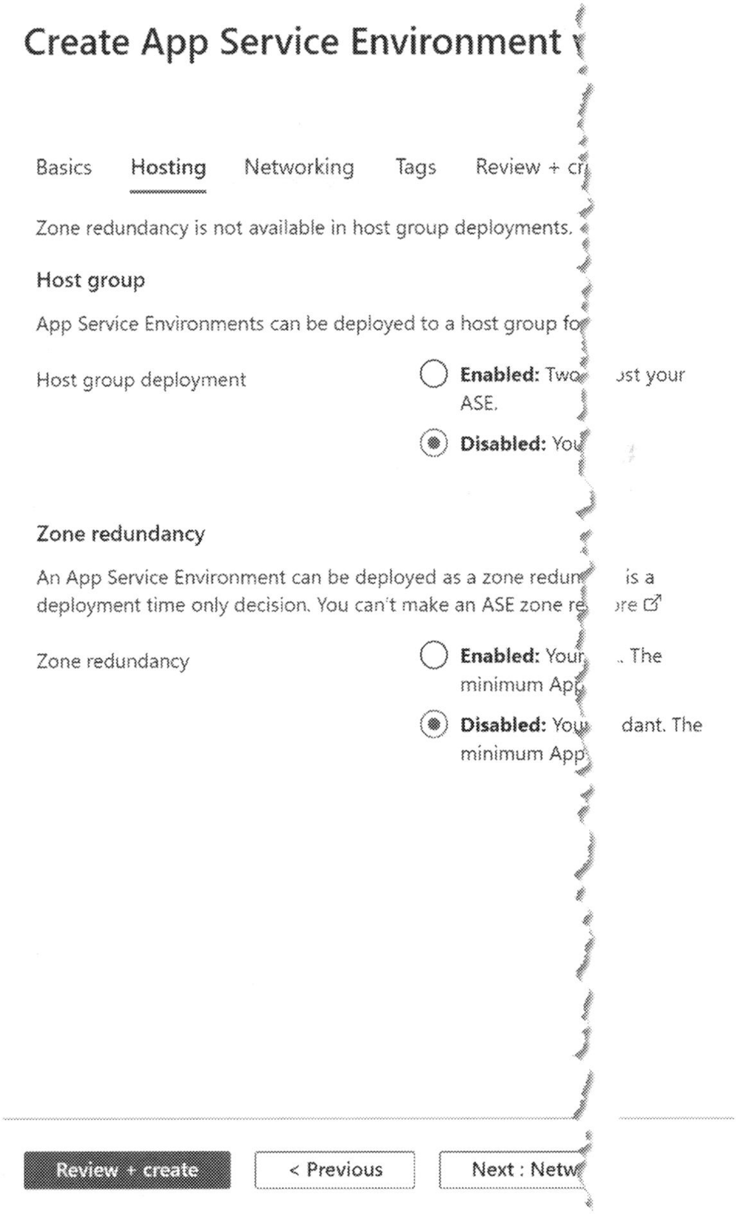

Create App Service Environment

Basics   **Hosting**   Networking   Tags   Review + cr

Zone redundancy is not available in host group deployments.

Host group

App Service Environments can be deployed to a host group fo

Host group deployment

○ **Enabled:** Two   ust your
ASE.

◉ **Disabled:** You

Zone redundancy

An App Service Environment can be deployed as a zone redun   is a
deployment time only decision. You can't make an ASE zone re   ore ☐

Zone redundancy

○ **Enabled:** Your   . The
minimum App

◉ **Disabled:** You   dant. The
minimum App

| Review + create | < Previous | Next : Netw |

Figure 10-5. *ASE hosting*

We can create a new virtual network for the ASE. You need to provide a name and region. The address block will be automatically selected (see Figure 10-6).

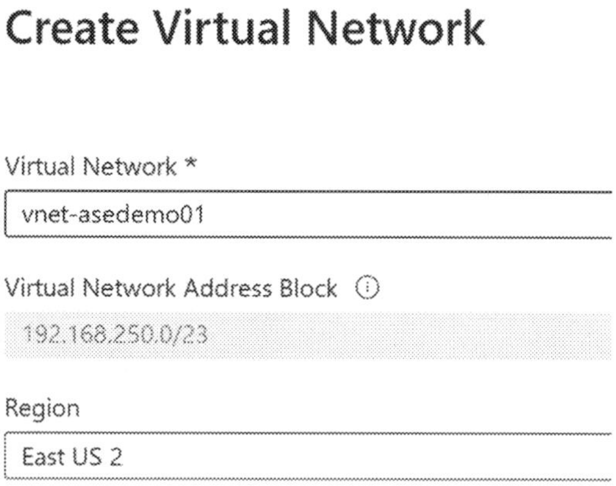

Create Virtual Network

Virtual Network *

vnet-asedemo01

Virtual Network Address Block ⓘ

192.168.250.0/23

Region

East US 2

Figure 10-6. *ASE vNet*

We need to define a subnet name as well for the ASE. In the subnet the address block will be with /24 CIDR providing 256 addresses in the subnet of the ASE (see Figure 10-7).

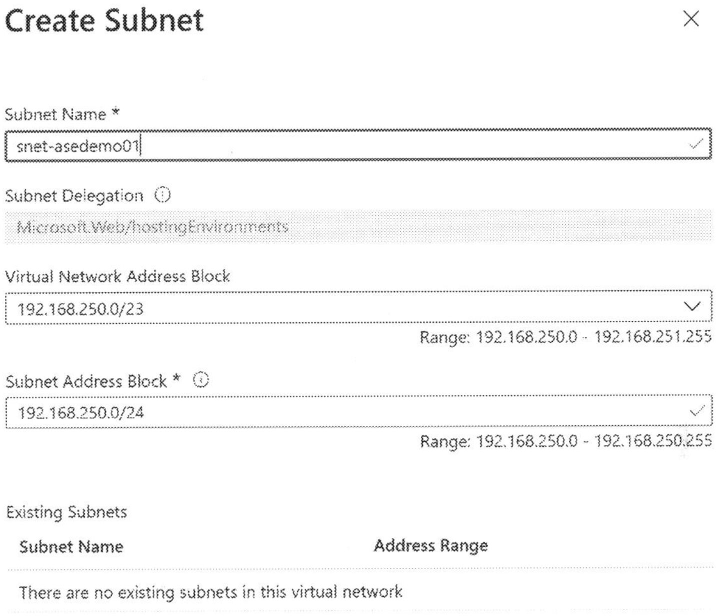

Create Subnet   ✕

Subnet Name *

| snet-asedemo01| | ✓ |

Subnet Delegation ⓘ

Microsoft.Web/hostingEnvironments

Virtual Network Address Block

| 192.168.250.0/23 | ∨ |

Range: 192.168.250.0 - 192.168.251.255

Subnet Address Block * ⓘ

| 192.168.250.0/24 | ✓ |

Range: 192.168.250.0 - 192.168.250.255

Existing Subnets

| Subnet Name | Address Range |

There are no existing subnets in this virtual network

Figure 10-7. *Subnet for ASE*

You can provide tags for the ASE of required and review all configurations before creating the ASE. Click on the create button to create the ASE (see Figure 10-8).

Figure 10-8. *Creating ASE*

It might take an hour or two to get your ASE deployment to complete. Let's explore the created ASE.

In the IP addresses blade, we can see that the inbound IP address and the outbound IP addresses are defined and virtual network and subnet association are visible (see Figure 10-9).

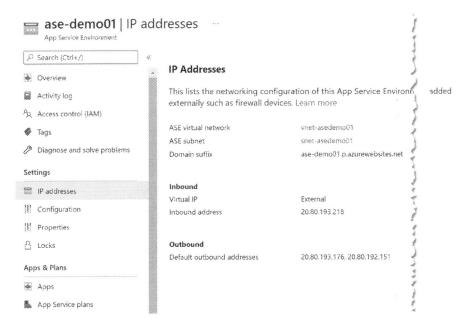

Figure 10-9. *ASE IP addresses*

If we check the Apps or App Service plans blades, we will see that no apps or plans have been added yet. The same information is shown in the overview page of the ASE (see Figure 10-10).

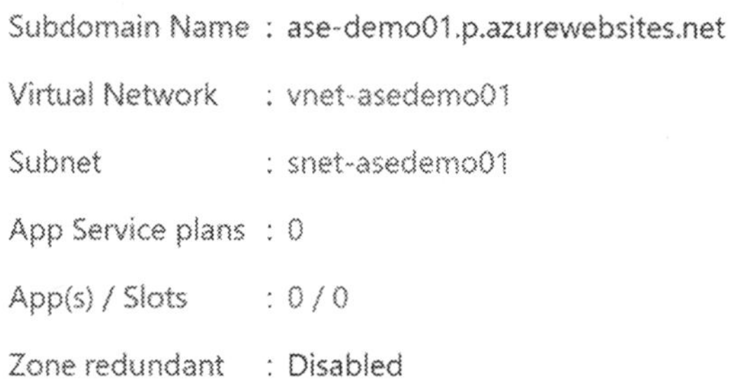

Subdomain Name : ase-demo01.p.azurewebsites.net
Virtual Network : vnet-asedemo01
Subnet : snet-asedemo01
App Service plans : 0
App(s) / Slots : 0 / 0
Zone redundant : Disabled

Figure 10-10. *ASE overview*

If we have a look at the resource group where we have set up the ASE, we can see that the ASE and the virtual network are available as resources (see Figure 10-11).

Resources
Filter for any field...
Showing 1 to 2 of 2 records.
Name
Type
ase-demo01
App Service Environment
vnet-asedemo01
Virtual network

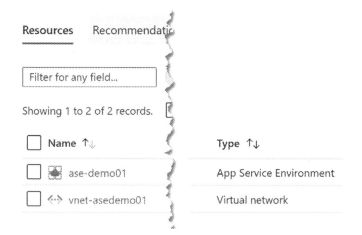

Figure 10-11. *Resources*

We have discussed the steps in setting up an ASE in this lesson.

Lesson 10.2: Creating Apps in App Service Environment

In the previous lesson we have created an ASE. The next step is to understand how we can deploy app service plans and apps to the ASE. If you explore the apps or app service plan blades on ASE, you will not see a way to add your apps or plans to ASE from those blades (see Figure 10-12).

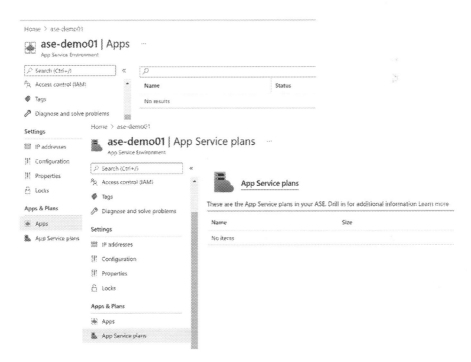

Figure 10-12.   *App service plans and apps in ASE*

Let's get started with creating an app service plan in the ASE to understand the steps. Search for an app service plan and click on app service plans in the Azure portal (see Figure 10-13).

217

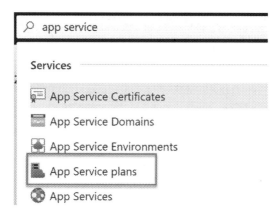

Figure 10-13. *Searching app service plans*

Click create to get started with app service plan creation (see Figure 10-14).

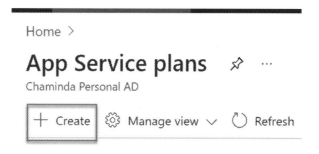

Figure 10-14. *Creating app service plan*

In the app service plan create window, instead of selecting the general Azure region, you need to select your ASE as the region. The resource group can be the same resource group your ASE is created in, or it can be a different resource group within the subscription of your ASE (see Figure 10-15).

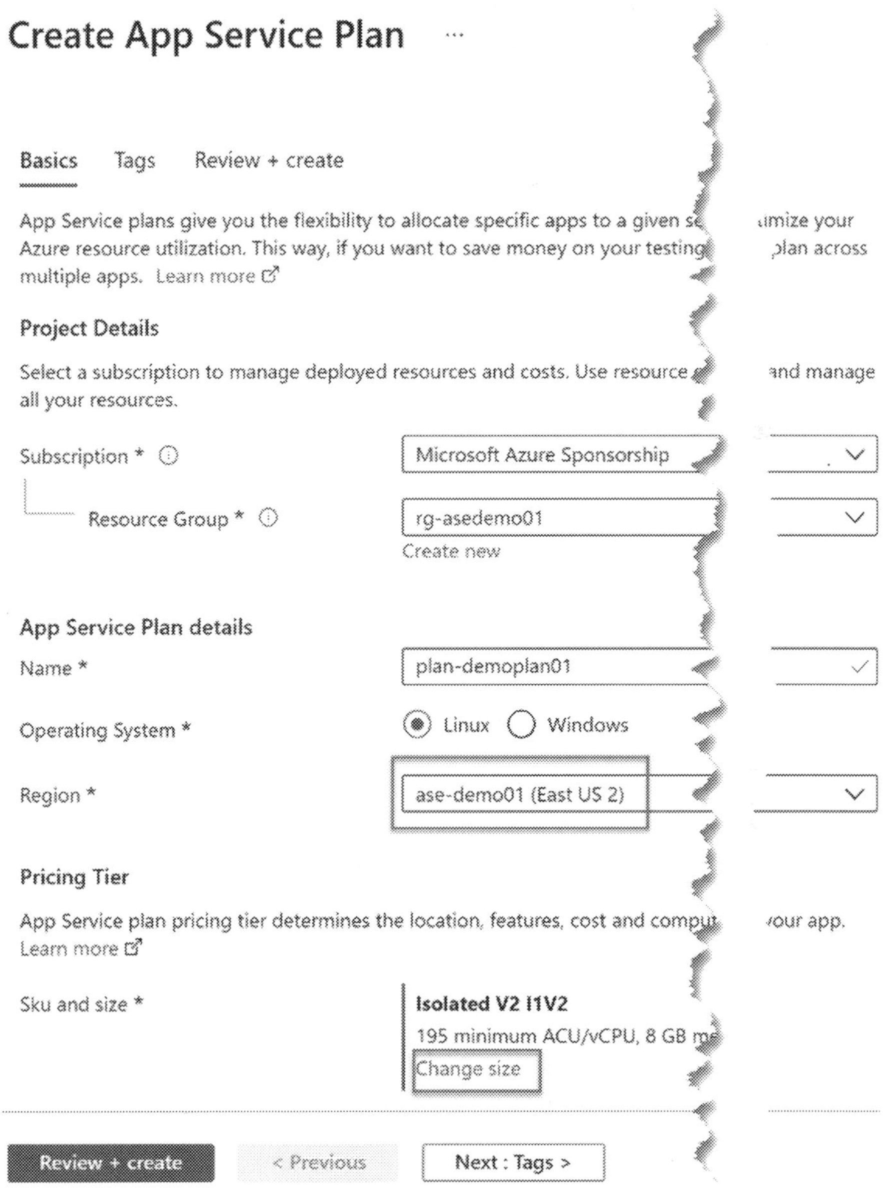

Create App Service Plan ...

Basics   Tags   Review + create

App Service plans give you the flexibility to allocate specific apps to a given se   imize your
Azure resource utilization. This way, if you want to save money on your testing   plan across
multiple apps. Learn more ☐

Project Details

Select a subscription to manage deployed resources and costs. Use resource   and manage
all your resources.

Subscription * ⓘ | Microsoft Azure Sponsorship | ∨

└──── Resource Group * ⓘ | rg-asedemo01 | ∨
                                     Create new

App Service Plan details

Name * | plan-demoplan01 | ✓

Operating System *   ◉ Linux   ○ Windows

Region * | ase-demo01 (East US 2) | ∨

Pricing Tier

App Service plan pricing tier determines the location, features, cost and comput   our app.
Learn more ☐

Sku and size *   **Isolated V2 I1V2**
                                    195 minimum ACU/vCPU, 8 GB m
                                    Change size

[Review + create]   [< Previous]   [Next : Tags >]

Figure 10-15. *Planning in ASE*

Click on change size in the app service plan create window (see Figure 10-15), and you will be able to see you are only allowed to select the pricing options in Isolated plans, because ASE is an isolated environment (see Figure 10-16).

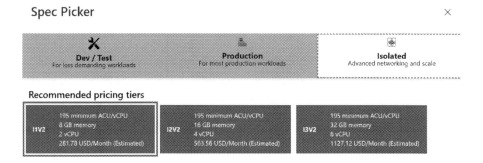

Figure 10-16. *ASE plan sizes*

Proceed with your review and create the plan. You will be able to see the plan appear in your ASE (see Figure 10-17).

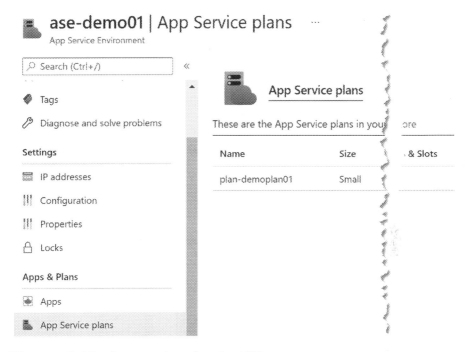

Figure 10-17. *App service plan in ASE*

Now let's see how we can create an app in ASE. You can even create the app in a different resource group from ASE resource group within the subscription. Similar to the app service plan, you need to select the region as ASE in the new app. Once you select ASE as the region you can utilize the previously created app service plan in ASE, or create a new plan with a different isolated size if necessary (see Figure 10-18).

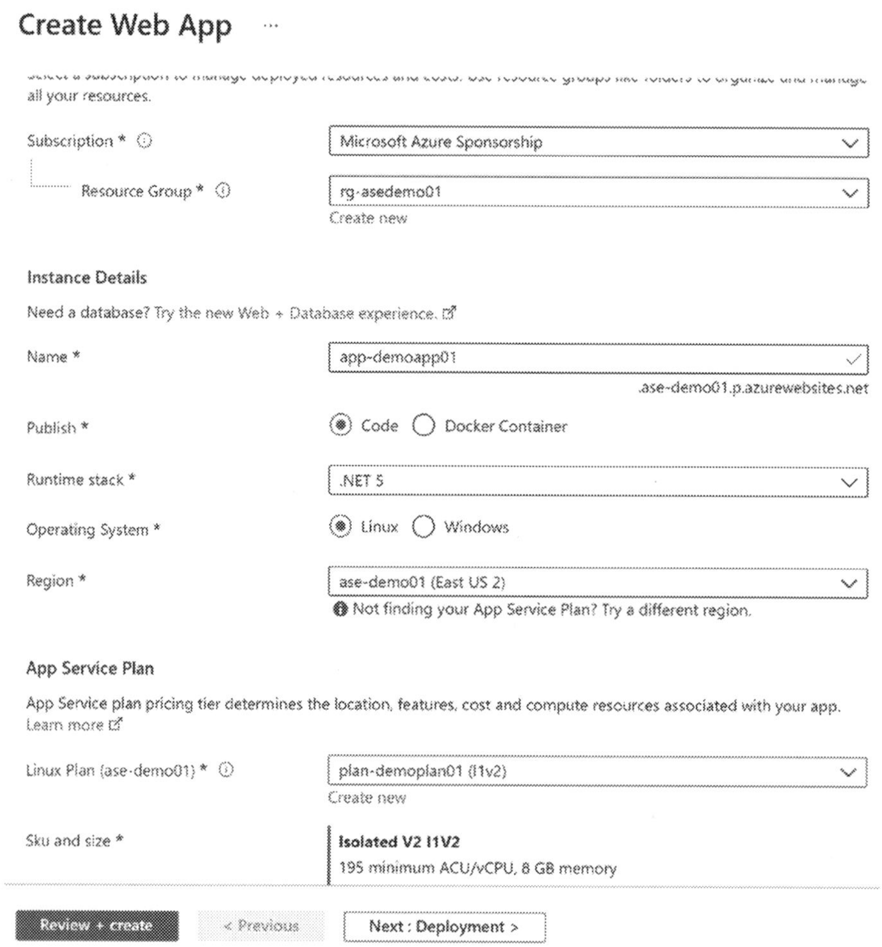

Create Web App   ...

Select a subscription to manage deployed resources and costs. Use resource groups like folders to organize and manage all your resources.

Subscription * ⓘ	Microsoft Azure Sponsorship ⌄
⌐⋯⋯ Resource Group * ⓘ	rg-asedemo01 ⌄
	Create new

Instance Details

Need a database? Try the new Web + Database experience. ⌐

Name *	app-demoapp01 ✓
	.ase-demo01.p.azurewebsites.net
Publish *	⦿ Code ◯ Docker Container
Runtime stack *	.NET 5 ⌄
Operating System *	⦿ Linux ◯ Windows
Region *	ase-demo01 (East US 2) ⌄
	❶ Not finding your App Service Plan? Try a different region.

App Service Plan

App Service plan pricing tier determines the location, features, cost and compute resources associated with your app. Learn more ⌐

Linux Plan (ase-demo01) * ⓘ	plan-demoplan01 (I1v2) ⌄
	Create new
Sku and size *	**Isolated V2 I1V2**
	195 minimum ACU/vCPU, 8 GB memory

Review + create	< Previous	Next : Deployment >

Figure 10-18.   Creating web app in ASE

Once the app is created, you can see that it is available in the ASE (see Figure 10-19).

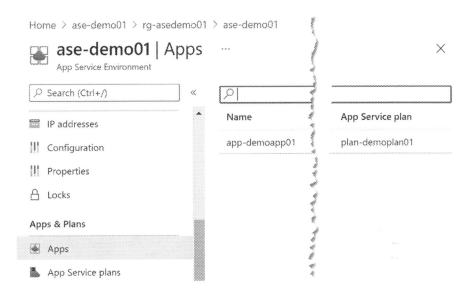

Figure 10-19. *App in ASE*

We have explored the steps to add an app service plan and web app to ASE. You can even add a function app using similar steps to the app service environment. In a function app create page, you can select the ASE as the region (see Figure 10-20).

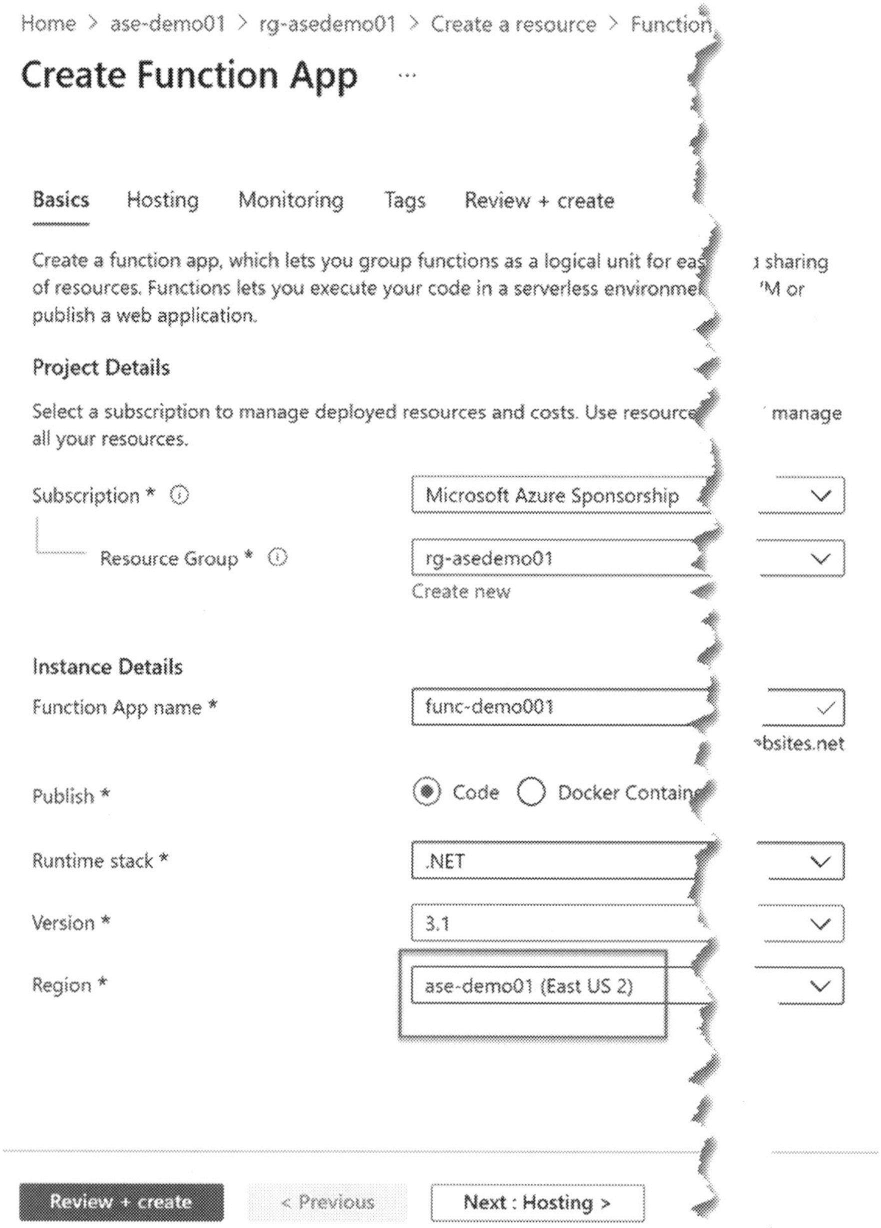

Home > ase-demo01 > rg-asedemo01 > Create a resource > Function

Create Function App   ...

Basics   Hosting   Monitoring   Tags   Review + create

Create a function app, which lets you group functions as a logical unit for eas   sharing of resources. Functions lets you execute your code in a serverless environme   'M or publish a web application.

Project Details

Select a subscription to manage deployed resources and costs. Use resource   manage all your resources.

Subscription * ⓘ	Microsoft Azure Sponsorship ∨
Resource Group * ⓘ	rg-asedemo01 ∨
	Create new

Instance Details

Function App name *	func-demo001 ✓
	ˑbsites.net
Publish *	⦿ Code ◯ Docker Contain
Runtime stack *	.NET ∨
Version *	3.1 ∨
Region *	ase-demo01 (East US 2) ∨

Review + create   < Previous   Next : Hosting >

Figure 10-20. *Creating function app in ASE*

In the hosting tab you can select the existing app service plan that is in the ASE, or create a new plan with isolated pricing (see Figure 10-21).

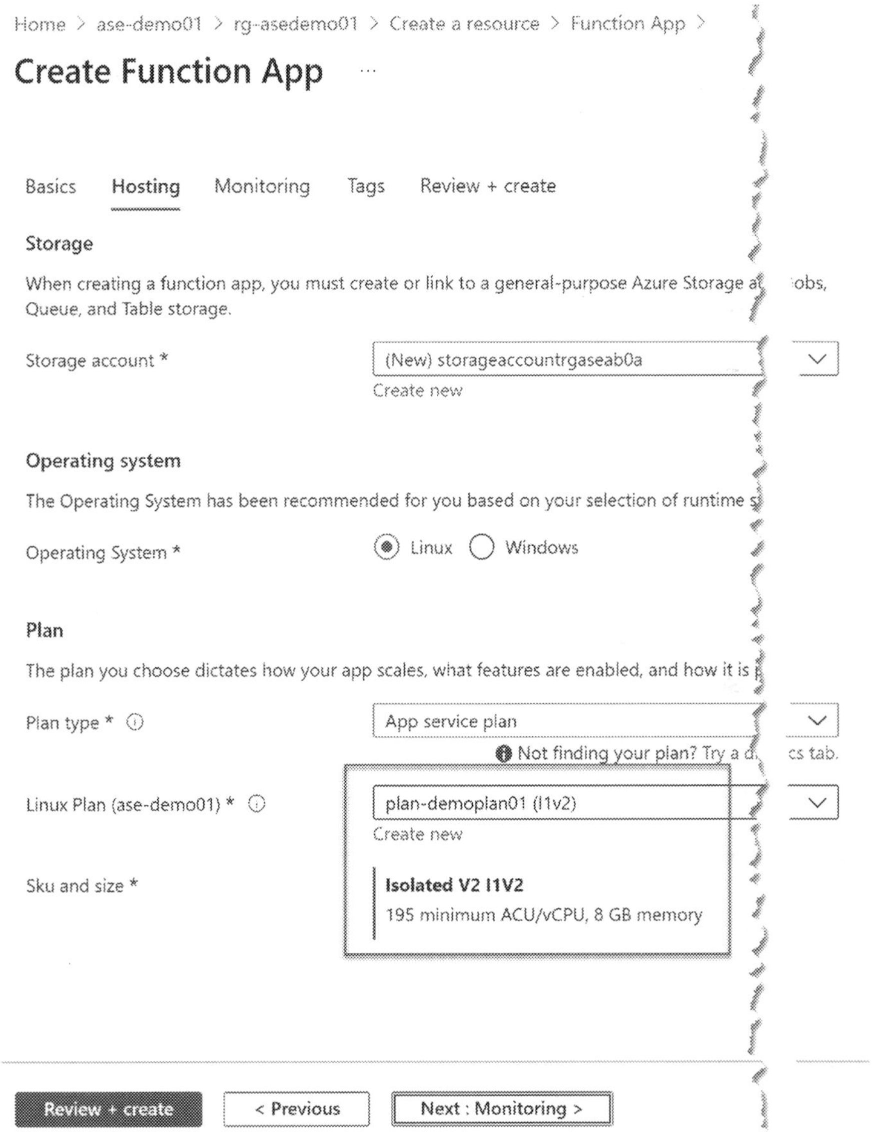

Home > ase-demo01 > rg-asedemo01 > Create a resource > Function App >

Create Function App   ...

Basics   **Hosting**   Monitoring   Tags   Review + create

Storage

When creating a function app, you must create or link to a general-purpose Azure Storage a͟ ͟obs, Queue, and Table storage.

Storage account *
| (New) storageaccountrgaseab0a | ∨ |
Create new

Operating system

The Operating System has been recommended for you based on your selection of runtime s͟

Operating System *   (●) Linux   (○) Windows

Plan

The plan you choose dictates how your app scales, what features are enabled, and how it is ͟

Plan type * ⓘ
| App service plan | ∨ |
❶ Not finding your plan? Try a d͟ cs tab.

Linux Plan (ase-demo01) * ⓘ
| plan-demoplan01 (I1v2) | ∨ |
Create new

Sku and size *
Isolated V2 I1V2
195 minimum ACU/vCPU, 8 GB memory

| Review + create | | < Previous | | Next : Monitoring > |

Figure 10-21. *Function app hosting in ASE*

The created function app is also available in the Apps list of the ASE (see Figure 10-22).

Figure 10-22. *Apps in ASE*

In this lesson, we have explored how to create apps in the app service environment.

Lesson 10.3: Deploying Apps in App Service Environment

In the previous lesson we have created apps in an ASE. Because an ASE is an isolated environment deploying applications, how we should be deploying applications to the app service environment is something worth exploring. In this lesson let's try to understand the steps in deploying a web app to an app hosted in ASE.

You are allowed to deploy to an app in ASE only within the virtual network of the ASE. Therefore, it is mandatory that your deployment pipeline actions are getting executed within the virtual network of ASE. In order to achieve this requirement, you need to deploy a self-hosted deployment agent to your ASE virtual network. You can set up a virtual machine in a subnet of the virtual network of the ASE. Then that virtual machine can be deployed with, for example, Azure DevOps hosted agent if you are using Azure DevOps to create your deployment pipelines. If it is GitHub, you can set up a self-hosted GitHub action runner in the virtual machine (see Figure 10-23).

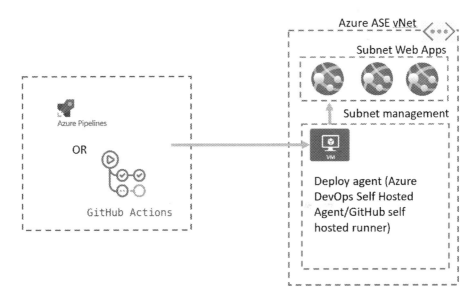

Figure 10-23. *Application deployment for ASE apps*

You need to allow the self-hosted agent or runner machine to have access to Azure DevOps or GitHub in order to obtain the packages to deploy and instructions to deploy based on the pipeline setup for deployment. The virtual machine in the same virtual network of the ASE will be able to reach the deployment URLs of the web apps to deploy the packages supplied by the deployment pipeline.

As you can see from the level of isolation required even for deploying to Apps in ASE, it is pretty much secure. Unlike public web apps, the web apps in ASE will be fully secured in isolation inside a virtual network by default. If a VPN is made from the ASE virtual network to your corporate network, the web apps in ASE will only be available within your corporate network boundary. For this setup ideally you should deploy the ASE with only an internal IP load balancer, as opposed to what we have done in lesson 2 of this chapter.

Even when you want to expose the web app in ASE publicly, it is recommended that you deploy load balancer with only internal IP and then add an application gateway web application firewall (WAF) to protect and expose it to the public with an additional layer of security.

In this lesson we have discussed the deployment consideration in web apps in an ASE.

Summary

In this chapter we have discussed the fully isolated app service environment deployment option in Azure to deploy web and function apps. We also explored how to set up ASE and set up apps inside ASE. The deployment considerations were described to give you an idea of the secure nature of the ASE-based web apps.

In this book, we have explored the security aspect in Azure PaaS services with all the basic details required to get started. The service security aspects, limitations, and enhancing options to ensure your application and data surety is described throughout this book.

Index

A

© Pushpa Herath 2022
P. Herath, *Azure Cloud Security for Absolute Beginners,*
https://doi.org/10.1007/978-1-4842-7860-4

Printed in the United States
by Baker & Taylor Publisher Services